ERNEST MANDEL

INTRODUCTION MARXISM

INTERNATIONAL
Series

Introduction to Marxism

Introduction to Marxism

Ernest Mandel

Translated by Louisa Sadler

First published in English as
From Class Society to Communism —
and Introduction to Marxism in 1977
By Inks Links Ltd.

Second edition, improved and with new material :
Introduction to Marxism,
published by Ink Links Ltd.,
271, Kentish Town Road,
London NW5 2JS

Introduction to Marxism
Copyright @ 1979 by Ernest Mandel

ISBN 0 906133 009 Cloth
ISBN 0 906133 025 Paper

Set by F.I. Litho Ltd., 328 Upper Street,
London N1 2XQ
Printed and bound by Whitstable Litho,
Millstrood Road, Whitstable, Kent.

Contents

From Class Society to Communism is the first in a series of titles to be published by Ink Links in association with *International*, the quarterly theoretical journal of the International Marxist Group (British section of the Fourth International).

   International regularly carries articles by Ernest Mandel and other noted revolutionary Marxists such as Denise Avenas, Tariq Ali, Robin Blackburn, Norman Geras, Dick Roberts, and Pierre Frank (whose book *The Fourth International: A Contribution to the History of the Trotskyist Movement* will appeared as the second title in this series in June 1978). Recent issues of *International* have also included interviews with Nicos Poulantzas and Fernando Claudin, as well as an ongoing debate with representatives of the Communist Party of Great Britain.

   For more details about the journal, subscriptions etc., write to: *International*, c/o Relgocrest Ltd., 328/9 Upper Street, London N.1 (annual subscription £3/$8: all cheques/money orders should be made out to Relgocrest Ltd.).

Foreword

This introduction to Marxism is the result of numerous experiences in giving educationals to young militants at various times in the last 15 years. It arises out of such pedagogical needs as we have noticed, and these can vary from country to country, from milieu to milieu. This introduced in no way pretends to be a 'model'.

Though it contains the basic elements of the theory of historical materialism, of Marxist economic theory, of the history of the workers movement and the problems of strategy and tactics for the workers movement in our times, it also contains an 'innovation' which might at first sight appear rather staggering: both the chapter on materialist dialectics and the chapter which systematically explains the theory of historic materialism are to be found at the end and not the beginning of the book.

This is not, of course, a 'revision of method' but a pedagogic formula drawn from practical observation: an explanation of dialectics in Marxism is more fitted to a course for the education of cadres than for the first initiation of militants, who assimilate theory better when it is presented in the most concrete form possible. It is therefore preferable to start off with notions which are immediately verifiable — social inequality, the class struggle, capitalist exploitation — and to come to the more abstract and fundamental concept of dialectics as the universal logic of motion and contradiction once we have clarified the movement of contemporary society and the contradictions which tear it apart.

This is not a final option, as it is based on personal teaching experience. It goes without saying that other experiences could lead to different conclusions. We are ready to return to the more traditional structure of an 'Introduction to Marxism' if it can be shown, from the evidence of practical experience, that such a method of explanation allows inexperienced militants to assimilate more easily the essence of Marxism. For the moment, we take leave to doubt it.

E.M.

Chapter 1

Social Inequality and Social Struggle Throughout History

1. Social inequality in contemporary capitalist society

A pyramid of wealth and social power exists in all capitalist countries. In the USA, a Senate Commission has estimated that less than one per cent of American families possess 80 per cent of all shares in companies, and that 0.2 per cent of families possess more than two-thirds of these shares. In Britain, in 1973, the richest one per cent of the population held 28 per cent of all marketable wealth; and the richest five per cent, 50.5 per cent of that wealth (these figures, however, strongly understate the concentration of wealth because they include private dwellings which, for a large part of the population, are not 'marketable wealth' but necessary living conditions). In Belgium one third of the citizens are at the bottom of this pyramid, possessing nothing other than what they earn and spend, year in, year out; they have no savings and no assets. Four per cent of the citizens occupy the top of this pyramid, owning *half* the private wealth of the nation. Less than one per cent of Belgians own more than half the stocks and shares in the country. Among these, 200 families control the big holding societies which dominate the whole of the nation's economic life. In Switzerland, one per cent of the population possess more than 67 per cent of the privately owned wealth.

Inequality of revenue and wealth is not only an economic fact. It implies inequality in chances of survival and death. In Great Britain before the Second World War, the infant mortality rate in the families of unskilled workers was double that in bourgeois families. Official statistics indicate that in France in 1951, infant mortality expressed in deaths per 1,000 births was 19.1 in the liberal professions, 23.9 among employers, 28.2 among commercial employees, 34.5 among tradespeople, 36.4 among artisans (craft workers), 42.5 among skilled workers, 44.9 among peasants and agricultural workers, 51.9 among semi-skilled workers, 61.7 among unskilled and manual workers. The proportional differences had hardly changed ten years later, although the infant mortality rate had fallen in each category.

Recently the conservative Belgian daily *La Libre Belgique* published a distressing study concerning language formation in the child. This study confirms that the handicap a child in a poor family often suffers during the first two years of its life, and the subsequent cultural under-development imposed by class society, produce lasting consequences with regard to the possibility of handling abstract concepts and assimilating scientific knowledge; consequences which a non-compensatory 'egalitarian' education cannot neutralise. It is an unfortunate fact that social inequality still stifles the development of thousands of Mozarts, Shakespeares and Einsteins among the children of the people even in the epoch of the 'welfare state'.

Nowadays it is not enough just to take stock of the social inequalities which exist in each country. It is even more important to take into account the inequality between a small handful of advanced countries (from the point of view of industrialisation) and the majority of humanity, living in the so-called under-developed countries (colonial and semi-colonial countries).

The USA accounts for nearly half of the industrial production and consumes more than half of a great number of primary industrial materials in the capitalist world. Five hundred and fifty million Indians have less steel and electrical energy at their disposal than nine million Belgians. The real *per capita* income in the poorest countries of the world is only eight per cent of the *per capita* income in the richest countries. Sixty-seven per cent of the world's population receive only 15 per cent of the world revenue. In India in 1970, 20 times as many women per 100,000 births died in childbirth as in Britain.

As a result an Indian's daily calorie intake is only half the daily intake in the West. Average life expectancy, which in the West is more than 65 years, and in some countries reaches

70 years, is barely 30 in India.

2 Social inequality in previous societies

Social inequality similar to that existing in the capitalist
world can be noted in all the previous societies which have
succeeded one another during the course of history, that is,
during that period of humanity's existence on earth of which
we have written accounts.

Here is a description of the misery of French peasants
towards the end of the Seventeenth Century, taken from the
French writer La Bruyère's book *The Characters:* 'One sees
certain savage animals, both male and female, scattered
about the countryside, black, livid and burnt all over by the
sun, attached to the earth which they grub up and turn over
with an invincible stubbornness. They have a sort of
articulated voice, and when they stand up on their feet, they
show a human face. They are in fact men. At night they retire
into dens, where they live off black bread, water and roots.'

Compare this picture of the peasants of the epoch to the
dazzling feasts given by Louis XIV at the court of Versailles,
to the luxury of the nobility and the squanderings of the
financiers. It is a striking image of social inequality.

In medieval society, which was dominated by serfdom, the
noble lord most often had half the labour or half the harvest
of the peasant-serfs at his disposal. Most lords had hundreds
if not thousands of serfs on their lands. Each lord therefore
profited every year from hundreds if not thousands of
peasants.

It was the same in the various societies of the classical East
(Egypt, Sumeria, Babylon, Persia, India, China, etc.),
societies based on agriculture, but in which the owners of the
land were either lords, temples or kings (represented by
scribes who were agents of the royal treasury).

The 'Satire of the Professions', written in the Egypt of the
Pharaohs, 3,500 years ago, has left us with an image of the
peasants exploited by these royal scribes, compared to
harmful beasts and parasites by the disgruntled cultivators.

As for Ancient Greece and Rome, their society was based
on slavery. That culture was able to reach a high level was
partly due to the fact that the citizens were able to

devote a large portion of their time to political, cultural, artistic and sporting pursuits, while the manual work was left to the slaves.

3 Social inequality and class inequality

Social inequality is not necessarily class inequality. For example, the pay differential between an unskilled worker and a highly skilled worker does not make these two people members of different social classes.

Class inequality is an inequality which is rooted in the structure of economic life, which corresponds to different economic functions, and which is perpetuated and accentuated by the principal social and legal institutions of the period.

A few examples will make this definition clearer.

To become a big capitalist in Belgium, you need to invest at least a million francs of capital for every worker employed. For a small factory employing 200 workers, a capital of at least 200 million francs is needed. The net earnings of a worker are rarely more than 200,000 francs a year. A worker who worked 50 years without spending a penny of their wages would still not have enough money to become a capitalist. Wage-labour, which is one of the basic characteristics of the structure of the capitalist economy, therefore constantly reproduces the division of capitalist society into two fundamentally different classes: the working class, which can never become the owner of the means of production by means of its earnings; and the capitalist class, which owns the means of production and expands this ownership through a reinvestment of part of its profits.

It is true that, besides the capitalists, some technicians become company directors. But a university education is needed. Over the last few decades only between five and seven per cent of Belgian students have been the daughters and sons of workers. It is the same in most imperialist countries.

Social institutions close all access for the workers to capitalist property, both because of their earnings and because of the system of higher education. These institutions maintain, conserve and perpetuate the class division of society as it exists today. Even in the USA, where examples of the 'sons of upstanding workers who became millionaires because they worked hard for it' are often complacently cited, an inquiry has shown that 90 per cent of the top managers of important companies come from the middle and big bourgeoisie.

Therefore throughout history we see social inequality crystallised into *class inequality*. In each society we can pick out a productive class which supports the whole of society through its labour, and a dominant class which lives off other people's work:

Peasants and priests, lords and scribes in the Eastern Empires;

Slaves and slave-owners in Ancient Greece and Rome;

Serfs and feudal lords in the Middle Ages;

Workers and capitalists in bourgeois society.

4 *Social inequality in human prehistory*

But history only covers a short period of human life in our planet. It is preceded by prehistory, which is the epoch in humanity's existence when writing and civilisation were still unknown. Until a recent date or even until our own time, primitive people remained in prehistoric conditions. During the best part of prehistoric existence, class inequality was unknown to humanity.

We can understand the fundamental difference between such a primitive community and class society by examining some of the institutions of these communities.

Several anthropologists have mentioned a custom which is found among many primitive peoples, which consists of organising plentiful feasts after the harvests. The anthropologist Margaret Mead has described these feasts among the Papuan tribe of Arapech (New Guinea). Those who have gathered in an above average harvest invite all their family and neighbours, and the festivities continue until most of the surplus has been consumed. Margaret Mead adds: 'These feasts represent an adequate way of preventing any individual accumulation of riches.'

The anthropologist Asch studied the customs and special system of the Hopi tribe, which lives in the southern USA. In contrast to our society, the principle of individual competition is considered morally reprehensible by this society. Hopi children never keep score, or know who has 'won' in their games and sports.

While agriculture, which occupies a set terrain, is the principal economic activity of primitive communities which are not yet divided into classes, there is often no longer any collective exploitation of the earth. Each family receives fields for work for a certain period. These fields are frequently redistributed to avoid favouring this or that member of the community more than the others. Pastures and woods are exploited in common. This *village community* system, which is based on the absence of private ownership of the land, is found at the origin of agriculture among nearly all the peoples of the world. It shows that at that time, society was not yet divided into classes at the village level.

The generally accepted view holds that social inequality is rooted in the inequality of individual talents or capacities, and that the class division of society is the product of humanity's 'innate egoism' and therefore a result of 'human nature'. This view has no scientific basis. The exploitation of one social class by another is the product of the historical evolution of society, and not of human nature. It has not always existed. It will not always survive. There have not always been rich and poor. There will not always be.

5 *Historical examples of revolt against social inequality*

Class society and the private ownership of the land and other means of production are therefore in no way the products of human nature, but of the society's evolution, of its economic and social institutions. We can see why they came about and how they will disappear.

In fact, humanity has shown its nostalgia for the ancient community life of clan or tribal communism since the class division of society first appeared. This is expressed in the much dreamed of 'Golden Age' at the very beginning of human existence, a dream described by classical Chinese authors as well as Greek and Latin authors. Virgil explicitly states that at the time of this Golden Age harvests were shared in common, which implies that private property did not exist.

Many famous philosophers and scholars have thought that the class division of society represented the source of social malaise, and elaborated projects for its replacement.

The Greek philosopher Plato characterised the origin of the ills from which society suffers like this: 'Even the smallest town is divided in two parts, the town of the poor and that of the rich, which are opposed as if in a state of war.'

The Jewish sects which grew up at the beginning of our era, and the Founding Fathers of the Christian Church who followed the same tradition in the Third to Fifth Centuries, were equally strong partisans of a return to the community of goods. St. Barnabas wrote: 'Never speak of your property, for if you partake of spiritual things in common it is all the more necessary to hold material goods in common.' St. Cyprian set forth many entreaties in favour of the egalitarian distribution of goods among men. St. John Chrysostomus was the first to say: 'Property is theft.' Even St. Augustine at first saw that the origin of social strife and social violence is private property, but later modified this view.

This tradition continued throughout the Middle Ages, mainly with St. Francis of Assisi and the precursors of the Reformation: the Albigensians, Cathari, Wyclif, etc. This is what the Englishman John Ball, a pupil of Wyclif, said in the Fourteenth Century: 'Slavery must be abolished and all men must be equal. Those who call themselves our masters consume what we produce....They owe their luxury to our labour.'

Finally we see these projects for an egalitarian society become more precise in the modern epoch with Thomas More's *Utopia* (English), Campanella's *The City of the Sun* (Italian), the works of Vaurasse d'Allais, and Morelly's *The Testament of Jean Meslier* and *The Code of Nature* (French).

Side by side with this spiritual revolt against social inequality, there have been innumerable actual revolts — that is, insurrections of oppressed classes against their oppressors. The history of all class societies is the history of the class struggles which rend them apart.

6 Class struggle in history

These struggles between the oppressed class and the exploiting class, or between various exploiting classes, take a variety of forms depending on the society you look at and the precise stage of its evolution.

There were a large number of revolts in the societies of the so-called 'Asiatic mode of production' (the Empires of the classical East).

In China, innumerable peasant uprisings stand out as landmarks in the history of the successive dynasties which reigned over the Empire. There were also a great number of peasant insurrections in Japan, especially in the Eighteenth Century.

In Ancient Greece and Rome, there was an uninterrupted series of slave revolts — the most well-known was led by Spartacus — which contributed considerably to the downfall of the Roman Empire. Among the free citizens there was a virulent struggle between a class of indebted peasants and the usurer-merchants — between those who had property and those who did not.

In the Middle Ages, class struggle set feudal lords against free communities based on petty commodity production, as well as artisans against merchants within these communities, and some urban artisans against peasants who lived near the towns. The most savage class struggles were those between the feudal nobility and the peasantry which was trying to throw off the feudal yoke, struggles which clearly took a revolutionary form with the Jacqueries in France, the uprising of Wat Tyler in England, that of the Hussites in Bohemia, and the peasant war in' Germany in the Sixteenth Century.

History between the Sixteenth and the Eighteenth Centuries is marked by class struggles between the nobility and the bourgeoisie, between master-artisans and journeymen, between rich bankers and traders on the one hand and the unskilled labourers of the towns on the other, etc. .... These struggles heralded the bourgeois revolutions, modern capitalism and the class struggle of the proletariat against the bourgeoisie.

Chapter 2
The Economic Sources of Social Inequality

1 Primitive communities based on poverty

During the major part of prehistoric existence, humanity lived in conditions of extreme poverty and could only obtain the food necessary for subsistence by hunting, fishing and fruit gathering.

Humanity lived off nature as a parasite, since it was unable to increase the natural resources which were the basis of its subsistence. Humanity could not control these resources.

Primitive communities are organised to guarantee collective survival in these extremely difficult conditions of existence. Everyone is obliged to take part in current production, and everyone's labour is necessary to keep the communities alive. The granting of material privileges to one part of the tribe would condemn another part to famine, would deprive it of the possibility of working normally, and would therefore undermine the conditions for collective survival. This is why social organisation, at this stage in the development of human societies, tends to maintain maximum equality within human communities.

After examining 425 primitive tribes, the English anthropologists Hobhouse, Wheeler and Ginsberg found a total absence of social classes amongst all the tribes who knew nothing about agriculture.

2 The neolithic revolution

It was only the development of techniques of agriculture and animal husbandry which modified this situation of fundamental poverty in any long term way. The technique of agriculture, the greatest economic revolution in humanity's existence, is attributable to women, as are a series of other important discoveries in pre-history (notably the techniques of pottery and weaving).

This started to take place around 15,000 B.C. in a few places in the world, most probably first of all in Asia Minor, Mesopotamia, Iran and Turkestan, gradually progressing into Egypt, India, China, North Africa and Mediterranean Europe. It is called the neolithic revolution because it happened during that part of the Stone Age when the principal tools of work were made of polished stone (the final epoch of the Stone Age).

The neolithic revolution allowed humanity to produce its food itself, and therefore to control more or less its own subsistence. Primitive humanity's dependence on the forces of nature was diminished. It permitted the building up of *food reserves*, which in turn released certain members of the community from the need to produce their own food. Thus a *certain economic division of labour* could develop, a specialisation of jobs, which increased the productivity of human labour. In primitive society there are as yet only the bare outlines of such specialisation. As one of the first Spanish explorers said in the Sixteenth Century about the American Indians: 'They (the primitive people) want to use all their time gathering together food, because if they used it in any other way, they would be overcome with hunger.'

3 Necessary product and social surplus product

The primitive conditions of social organisation were overturned as a result of the appearance of a large and permanent surplus of food. As long as this surplus was relatively small and scattered from village to village, it did not modify the egalitarian structure of the village community. It only provided nourishment for a few artisans and officials, similar to those who have been maintained by Hindu villages for thousands of years.

But once these surpluses are concentrated over great areas by military or religious chiefs, or once they become more abundant in the village thanks to the improvement of agricultural techniques, they can create the conditions for the appearance of social inequality. They can be used to feed prisoners captured in war or on pirate expeditions (who would hitherto have been killed for lack of food). These prisoners can be obliged to work for their captors in exchange for their food: that is how slavery came into existence in the world of Ancient Greece.

The same surplus can be used to nourish a population of priests, soldiers, officials, lords and kings. That is how the ruling classes appeared in the empires of the Ancient East — Egypt, Babylon, Iran, India, China.

A *social* division of labour then completes the *economic* division of labour (specialisation of productive skills). Social production no longer serves in its totality to fulfil the needs of the producers. It is henceforth divided into two parts:

— the *necessary product;* in other words, the means of subsistence for the producers without whose labour the whole society would collapse.

— the *social surplus product;* the surplus produced by the labourers and appropriated by the owning classes.

This is how the historian Heichelheim describes the appearance of the first towns in the ancient world: 'The population of the new urban centres is composed.... mainly of a superior layer living off taxes [that is, appropriating the surplus product of agricultural labour — EM], composed of priests, lords and nobles. Add to this the officials, employees and servants indirectly nourished by this superior layer.'

The appearance of distinct and antagonistic social classes — productive classes and ruling classes — thus gives birth to the state, which is the principal institution for the maintenance of the given social conditions — that is, social inequality. The division of society into classes is consolidated by the appropriation of the means of production by the possessing classes.

4 Production and accumulation

The formation of social classes, the appropriation of the social surplus product by one part of society, is the result of a *social struggle* and is only maintained by constant social struggle.

But at the same time it represents an inevitable stage in economic progress, as it permits the separation of the two fundamental economic functions — production and accumulation.

In primitive society, all healthy men and women are mainly occupied with the production of food. In these conditions they can give only a small amount of time to the fabrication and stockpiling of tools, to the learning of complicated techniques (for instance, metallurgy), to the systematic observation of natural phenomena, etc.

The production of a social surplus allows part of humanity to have enough *leisure time* to devote itself to all those activities that help *increase the social productivity of labour.*

These leisure time activities are fundamental to civilisation, to the development of the first scientific techniques (astronomy, geometry, hydrography, mineralogy, etc.), and of writing.

The separation of intellectual and manual labour, which is the product of these leisure time activities , accompanies the separation of society into classes.

The division of society into classes therefore represents a condition of historical progress for as long as society is too poor to allow all its members to dedicate themselves to intellectual labour (to accumulative functions). But a heavy price is paid for this progress. Up until the era of modern capitalism, only the ruling classes profited from the advantages of the growth in the social productivity of labour. In spite of all the technical and scientific progress of the 4,000 years which separate the beginnings of ancient civilisation from the Sixteenth Century, the situation of the Indian, Chinese, Egyptian, or even Greek and Slavonic peasants hardly changed at all during this time.

5 The reasons for the failure of all past egalitarian revolutions

As long as the surplus produced by human society, the social surplus product, is not sufficient to liberate the whole of humanity from repetitive, mechanical and tiring labour, any social revolution which tries to re-establish equality is condemned to failure. It can find only two solutions to social inequality:

(a) It can deliberately destroy any social surplus and return to extreme, primitive poverty. In this case, the reappearance of technical and economic progress would provoke the same social inequalities whose eradication had been sought.

(b) It can dispossess the old possessor class in favour of a new one.

That is essentially what happened with the insurrection of Roman slaves under Spartacus, with the first Christian sects and monasteries, the various insurrections under the Chinese Empire, the revolution of the Taborites in Fifteenth Century Bohemia, with the communist colonies established by the immigrants in America, etc.

Without pretending that the Russian Revolution ended up in the same situation, the reappearance today of accentuated social inequality in the USSR can fundamentally be explained by the poverty of Russia immediately after the revolution, by the insufficient level of development of the productive forces, and by the isolation of the revolution in a backward country after the failure of the revolution in Central Europe in the years 1918-1923.

An egalitarian society founded on abundance and not poverty — and that is the aim of socialism — can only be developed on the basis of an advanced economy in which the social surplus product is so high that it allows all producers to liberate themselves from tiring, routine labour, granting sufficient leisure time to the whole community so that they can collectively fulfil the managerial tasks of economic, social and political life (the function of accumulation).

Why has it taken 15,000 years of social surplus production for humanity to be able to experience the necessary expansion of production which allows us to envisage a socialist solution to social inequality? The answer lies in the fact that as long as the propertied classes appropriate the social surplus product in natural form, in the form of use values, their own consumption, *unproductive consumption*, imposes a limit to the growth of production that they wish to bring about.

The temples and kings of the Ancient East; the slave-owners of Ancient Greece and Rome; the Chinese, Indian, Japanese, Byzantine and Arab lords and merchants; the feudal nobles of the Middle Ages — none had any further interest in increasing production once they had amassed in their castles and palaces enough goods, *objets d'art* and luxurious clothes. There is an absolute limit to the possibilities of individual consumption and the acquisition of luxuries (for instance, the social surplus product in the feudal society of the Hawaian Isles took the exclusive form of food, and because of this, social prestige depended . . . on body weight).

It is only when the social surplus product takes the form of money — of surplus value — and when it no longer serves merely for the acquisition of consumer goods but also for that of means of production, that the new ruling class — the bourgeoisie — acquires an interest in the unlimited growth of production. Thereby the necessary social conditions are created for an application of all scientific discoveries to production — in other words, the conditions necessary for the appearance of modern industrial capitalism.

6 The oppression of women: first institutionalised form of social inequality

There was a transitional epoch between the primitive communist society of the horde and the clan, and the first forms of society based on the domination of one class over another (for example, slave society). This period was one where a propertied ruling class had not as yet fully emerged, but where developing social inequality was already institutionalised. We know of the existence of this type of society not merely through numerous remains and descriptions of the past, which survive notably in myths, legends, and so-called 'primitive' religions. We know of it also through the society based on tribal kinship relations which survives today in some of the regions of Black Africa, even though it is increasingly deformed by its inter-relationship with the class society which now predominates there.

This first institutionalised form of social inequality and oppression is that of women by men in primitive societies which have reached this stage in their development.

The oppression of women has not always existed. It is not the result of any 'biological destiny' weighing down on the female sex. On the contrary, there is abundant prehistoric evidence concerning primitive communist (clan) society showing that for a long time sexual equality was there the norm. There is insufficient data for us to be able to generalise this phenomenon throughout primitive humanity. But it is clear that, at least in a series of societies, women played a role which was even socially dominant. The widespread phenomenon of the 'fertility-goddess' as mistress of heaven, at the dawn of the agriculture invented by women, is enough to show that the general substitution of gods (and then of a single god) for this goddess cannot have been accidental. The revolution in heaven reflected a revolution brought about on earth. The overturning of religious ideas resulted from an overturning of social conditions, of the mutual relations between men and women.

At first sight it might seem paradoxical that the dominant economic role of women, summed up in the agricultural work they did in the fields (the Neolithic revolution), should little by little open up the era of their social subjection. But there is no real contradiction there.

With the growth of primitive agriculture, women became the main source of tribal wealth, doubly so: as the principal producers of food, and as child-bearers. For only on the basis of a more or less guaranteed supply of food is population growth no longer regarded as a threat but rather as a potential benefit. Women thereby become economically coveted, which they could not be in the epoch of hunting and fruit-gathering.

A series of social struggles and transformations had to be carried through, however, in order to bring about this subjection. Women had to be disarmed — in other words, the bearing of arms had to become a male monopoly. The numerous legends concerning the Amazons, which survive on all continents, show that this was not always so. Women's status also had to be drastically changed in terms of the rules regarding marriage and the socialisation of children, with the aim of ensuring the predominance of patriarchy.

The development and then consolidation of private property sees the patriarchal family gradually take on the final form that it has retained — despite successive modifications — throughout a large part of the history of class society. It

becomes itself an irreplaceable institution ensuring the consolidation of private property through inheritance and social
oppression in all its forms (including ways of thinking geared
to the blind obedience of orders 'from above'). It becomes
the cultural crucible for innumerable instances of discrimination against women in all spheres of social life. The ideological justifications and hypocritical prejudices which sustain
this discrimination have been an integral part of the dominant ideology of practically all the propertied classes which
have followed one another in history. Hence they have also
entered at least partially into the exploited classes' consciousness — including that of the modern proletariat under the
capitalist system and during the period after its overthrow.

Chapter 3
The State, Instrument of Class Domination

1 The social division of labour and the birth of the state

In primitive classless societies, administrative functions were carried out by all the members of the tribe. Everyone carried arms. Everyone took part in assemblies which took all decisions concerning the life of the community and the relations of the community with the outside world. Internal conflicts were also settled by the members of the community.

Of course, one should not idealise the situation within these primitive communities which lived under clan or tribal communism.

The society was very poor. Life was a constant struggle with the forces of nature. The morals, customs, and rules for the settlement of internal and external conflicts resulted, even though they were collectively applied, from ignorance, fear and magical beliefs. However, it is necessary to emphasise the fact that society collectively governed itself within the limits of its knowledge and possibilities.

It is therefore not true that the notions of 'society', 'collective human organisation' and 'the state' are practically identical and can be found mutually interlinked throughout humanity's existence. On the contrary, for thousands of years humanity lived in societies quite ignorant of the existence of a state.

The state was born when the functions which were previously undertaken by all members of a society became the prerogative of *a separate group of people*:

— an army distinct from the mass of armed citizens;

— judges who took over from the mass of citizens the task of judging their equals;

— hereditary chiefs, kings and nobles in place of representatives or leaders of a particular activity, elected

temporarily and always recallable by the collective;
— 'ideological producers' (priests, clerks, teachers, philosophers, scribes and mandarins) set apart from the rest of the community.

The birth of the state is therefore the product of a double transformation: the appearance of a permanent social surplus product, relieving a part of the society from the obligation to work in order to ensure its subsistence, and thus creating the *material conditions* for this part of society to specialise in the accumulative and administrative functions; and a social and political transformation permitting the exclusion of the rest of the community from the exercise of the political functions which had hitherto been everyone's concern.

2 The state in the service of the ruling classes

The fact that the functions which had been carried out by all the members of primitive communities became at a certain point in time the prerogative of a separate group of people indicates in itself that there are people *who profit from* this exclusion. It is the ruling classes who organise the exclusion of the members of the exploited and productive classes from the exercise of those functions which would allow them to abolish the exploitation imposed on them.

The example of the army and armament is the most convincing proof of this. The birth of the ruling classes is brought about through the appropriation of the social surplus product by a fraction of the society. The evolution which one finds at the origin of the birth of the state in the oldest Eastern Empires (Egypt, Mesopotamia, Iran, China, India, etc.) has been reproduced over the last few centuries in many African tribes and villages: gifts, services in the form of mutual aid, which were at first benevolently exchanged between all households, progressively become obligatory and are transformed into levies, taxes and forced labour.

But it is still necessary to make this requisitioning *secure*. This is mainly done through the constraint of arms. Groups of armed men — it matters little whether they be called soldiers, police, pirates or bandits — *compel* the cultivators and cattle breeders (later also the artisans and merchants) to give up a part of their production for the benefit of the ruling classes. To this end they carry arms and prevent the producers from being armed as well.

In Ancient Greece and Rome it was strictly forbidden for slaves to possess arms. It was the same for the serfs of the Middle Ages or the peasants in feudal Japan. The first slaves were, moreover, often prisoners of war who were kept alive, and the first exploited peasants were often inhabitants of conquered countries; in other words, they were the victims of *a process which disarms the producers and accords the monopoly of arms to conquerors, rulers and their retinue.*

In this sense, Engels is right to sum up the definition of the state with the formula: a body of armed men. Of course, the state fulfils functions other than that of arming the propertied classes and disarming the productive class. But, in the last analysis, its function is that of constraint exercised over one section of society by another. Nothing in history can justify the liberal bourgeois thesis that the state was born of a 'contract', a 'convention', freely engaged in by all the members of a community. On the contrary, everything confirms the fact that it is the product of a constraint of violence exercised by a few against the rest.

If the appearance of a state allows the ruling classes to maintain the appropriation of the social surplus, this same appropriation allows the members of the state apparatus to be paid. The more important this social surplus is, the more the state can bolster itself up with greater numbers of soldiers, officials and ideologists.

The development of the state in the feudal Middle Ages makes these relations particularly transparent. At the height of feudalism each feudal noble was 'in his domain' the head of the army, the tax collector, empowered to mint new currency, the administrator in chief, and director of the economy. But progressively, as feudal domains were extended, as a hierarchy was established among nobles, and dukes and barons emerged with power over considerable areas of land, it became impossible to exercise all these functions personally. This was even more true of kings and emperors.

Thus the characters incarnating the separation of these

functions emerged: seneschals, marshals, ministers, secre-
taries of state, etc. But a study of the meaning of words
reveals how ministers were originally the slaves or serfs of the
lord; that is to say, they were in a state of total dependency
on the ruling class.

3 Violent constraint and ideological integration

Although, in the last analysis, the state is a body of armed
men, and the power of the ruling class is based on violent
constraint, it cannot limit itself exclusively to this. Napoleon
Bonaparte said that you can do anything with a bayonet
except sit on it. A class society which only survived through
armed violence would find itself in a state of permanent civil
war — in other words, in a state of extreme crisis.

To consolidate the domination of one class over another for
any length of time, it is therefore absolutely essential that the
producers, the members of the exploited class, are brought to
accept the appropriation of the social surplus by a minority
as inevitable, permanent and just. That is why the state does
not only fulfil a repressive function, but also a function of
ideological integration. It is the 'ideological producers' who
make the fulfilment of this function possible.

Humanity is unique in that it cannot assure its survival
except by *social labour*, which implies social relations
between people.

These indispensable bonds imply the necessity of communication, of language, which permits the development of
consciousness, reflection, and the 'production of ideas'.
Thus all important actions in human life are accompanied by
reflections on these actions in people's heads.

But these reflections do not come about in a totally
spontaneous manner. Each individual doesn't just invent
new ideas. Most individuals think with the help of ideas
learnt in school or in church, and, in our times, with the help
of ideas borrowed from TV, radio, advertising and the
newspapers as well. The current production of ideas, and of
systems of ideas called ideologies, is therefore rather limited.
It is to a large extent also the monopoly of a small minority in
society.

In every class society *the dominant ideology is that of the ruling class.* This is the case essentially because the producers of ideology find themselves in material dependence on the owners of the social surplus product. In the Middle Ages, poets, painters, and philosophers were literally maintained by the nobility and the Church (itself the largest feudal landlord apart from the nobility). When the social and economic situation changed, the merchants and rich bankers appeared as the patrons of literary, philosophical and artistic works. The material dependence is no less pronounced. It is not until the arrival of capitalism that ideological producers appear who are no longer directly dependent on the ruling class. They work for an open market on which, however, almost the only buyers are capitalists and the bourgeois state.

Whatever the dominant ideology, its function is that of stabilising the society as it is — in other words, of stabilising class rule. The *law* protects and justifies the predominant form of ownership. The *family* plays the same role. *Religion* teaches the exploited to accept their fate. The *predominant moral and political ideas* seek to justify the rule of the dominant class with the help of sophisms and half-truths (for example, the thesis of Goethe, formulated during and against the French Revolution, according to which the disorder provoked by the struggle against injustice would be worse than the injustice itself. Moral: do not change the established order).

4 Ruling ideology and revolutionary ideology

But if the *dominant* ideology of each epoch is that of the ruling class, this in no way means that the *only* ideas that exist in a given society are those of the ruling class. In general — and simplifying — each class society contains at least three major categories of ideas within it:

— the ideas reflecting the interests of the ruling class of the epoch, which are dominant;

— the ideas of the previous ruling classes, who have already been defeated and thrown out of power, but who continue to exercise an influence on people. This fact is due to *the force of inertia of consciousness, which always lags behind material reality*. The transmission and diffusion of ideas is partly independent of what is happening in the sphere of material production. They can therefore remain influenced by social forces which are no longer the predominant forces economically;

— the ideas of a new revolutionary class which is emerging and, although still dominated, has already begun the fight for its emancipation and must, at least partially, throw off the ideas of its oppressors before it can throw off the oppression itself.

The example of Nineteenth Century France is very typical. The bourgeoisie is the ruling class. It has its own thinkers, lawyers, ideologists, philosophers, moralists and writers from the beginning to the end of the century. The semi-feudal nobility have been overthrown as the ruling class by the French Revolution. They will not return to power with the Bourbon restoration of 1815. But their ideology, especially ultra-montane clericalism, will continue to exercise a profound influence for decades, not merely on the remains of the nobility, but also on parts of the bourgeoisie, and on certain layers of the petty bourgeoisie (peasants) and even of the working class.

Side by side with bourgeois ideology and semi-feudal ideology there has, however, already developed a proletarian ideology, first of all that of the supporters of Babeuf and of the Blanquists, then that of the Proudhonists and of the collectivists, which leads us to Marxism and the Paris Commune.

5 Social revolutions and political revolutions

The more stable a class society is, the less the domination of the ruling class is challenged, and the more class struggle is absorbed into limited conflicts which do not question the structure of that society, what Marxists call the basic *relations of production* or the *mode of production*. But the more the economic and social stability of a particular mode of production is shaken, the more the domination of the ruling class is being challenged, the more class struggle will develop to the point of posing the question of the *overthrow* of this domination — the question of a *social revolution*.

A social revolution breaks out when the exploited and

oppressed classes no longer accept this domination as inevitable, permanent and just; when they no longer allow themselves to be intimidated and repressed by the violent constraints of rulers, when they no longer accept the ideology justifying this rule, when they are gathering the material and moral forces necessary for the overthrow of the ruling class.

Profound economic transformations prepare such conditions. The existing social organisation and the given mode of production, which have allowed the productive forces and the material wealth of the society to develop during a certain period, have become a brake to their continued development. The expansion of production enters into collision with its social organisation, with the social relations of production. There lies the ultimate source of all the social revolutions in history.

A social revolution substitutes the rule of one class for that of another. It presupposes the elimination of the previous ruling class from state power. Every social revolution is accompanied by a political revolution. The bourgeois revolutions are in general characterised by the elimination of the absolute monarchy and its replacement by a political power in the hands of assemblies elected by the bourgeoisie. The Estates-General suppressed the power of Philip II of Spain in the revolution of the Netherlands. The English Parliament destroyed the absolutism of Charles I in the English revolution of 1649. The American Congress destroyed the domination of George III over the thirteen colonies. The various Assemblies of the French Revolution destroyed the power of the Bourbon monarchy.

But if every social revolution is at the same time a political revolution, every political revolution is not necessarily a social one. *A revolution which is only political* implies the replacement, by revolutionary means, of *one form of domination,* one *state form* of a class, *by another state form of the same class.*

Thus the French revolutions of 1830, 1848 and 1870 were political revolutions which successively installed the July Monarchy, the Second Republic, the Second Empire and the Third Republic, all different political forms of government of the same social class — the bourgeoisie. In general, political revolutions overthrow the state form of the same social class as a function of the predominant interests of the various layers and factions of that same class which succeed each other in power. But the fundamental mode of production is in no way overthrown by these revolutions.

6 Particularities of the bourgeois state

The modern bourgeoisie did not start from scratch in creating its state machine. It largely contented itself with taking over the state machinery of absolute monarchy and then remodelling it into an instrument which would serve its class interests.

The bourgeois state is distinct in that, apart from its repressive function and its ideological (integrationist) function, it also fulfils a function which is indispensable to the smooth running of the capitalist economy: that of guaranteeing the *general conditions of capitalist production*. Capitalist production is effectively generalised commodity production based on private property, and therefore on competition. This fact itself means that the collective interests of the bourgeoisie as a class cannot be identified with the interests of any one capitalist, even the richest. The state acquires a certain autonomy in order to be able to represent these collective interests; it is the 'ideal collective capitalist' (Engels).

Stable and equal conditions of law and security for every capitalist are necessary if the capitalist economy is to function in a normal, not to say an ideal manner. At the very least, a unified national market, a monetary system based on a certain number of national currencies, and a national and international system of acknowledged (i.e. written) law must exist. All these conditions do not spontaneously result from private production and capitalist competition. They are created by the bourgeois state.

When the bourgeoisie is economically prosperous and in ascendancy, sure of its social and political domination, it tends to reduce the economic functions of the state to the minimum we have just mentioned. In conditions where bourgeois rule is weakening and in decline, however, it tries on the contrary to extend these functions so as to make the state guarantee private profit.

Chapter 4

Mode of Production

1 Production for the satisfaction of needs, and production for exchange

In primitive society, and then within the village community born of the neolithic revolution, production was essentially based on the satisfaction of the needs of the productive collectivities. Exchange was only accidental, and affected only a tiny fraction of the products at the disposal of the community.

Such a form of production presupposes the deliberate organisation of labour. *As a consequence, labour is directly social.* Deliberate organisation of labour is not necessarily the same as conscious (and certainly not scientific) organisation. Many things may be left to chance, precisely because no thrust towards private enrichment presides over economic activity. Morals, ancestral habits, customs, rites, religion and magic can determine the alternance and rhythm of productive activities. But they are always essentially destined to satisfy the immediate needs of the collectivities, and not for exchange or enrichment as an end in itself.

A diametrically opposed form of economic organisation slowly emerges from this primitive community. Owing to progress in the division of labour, and the appearance of a certain stable surplus, the labour potential of the collectivity is progressively fragmented into units (big families, patriarchal families) working independently of each other. The *private character of labour* and the private ownership of the products of labour and even of the means of production gradually separate the members of the community one from another. This also prevents them from deliberately and immediately establishing economic relations amongst themselves. These units or individuals no longer have a direct relationship to each other in economic life. Their relations are formed *through the intermediary of the exchange of the products of their labour.*

The *commodity* is a product of social labour which is destined to be exchanged by its producer and not to be consumed by him or her, or by the immediate collectivity of which they are a part. The social situation is therefore fundamentally different from that in which the mass of products are destined to be immediately consumed by the collectivity which produced them. There are, of course, transitional cases (e.g. the so-called subsistence farms of our epoch, which sell a small surplus on the market). But the fundamental difference between a society in which production is essentially for the direct consumption of the producers, and one in which production is for exchange, is well caught in the malicious reply of the German socialist Ferdinand Lassalle to a liberal economist of his time: is it true that Mr Smith, an undertaker, would first of all manufacture coffins for his own use and that of the members of his household, and would sell only the surplus coffins he was left with....?

2 Petty commodity production

The production of commodities first appeared about ten to twelve thousand years ago in the Middle East, within the framework of the first fundamental division of labour between professional artisans and peasants — that is, after the appearance of the first towns. The economic organisation in which production for exchange by producers who remain masters of their conditions of production prevails is called petty commodity production.

Although there were many forms of petty commodity production, especially in Antiquity and in the Asiatic mode of production, it experienced its principal upsurge between the Fourteenth and Sixteenth Centuries in Northern and Central Italy and the Northern and Southern Netherlands (and to a lesser extent in England, France and Western Germany). This was as a result of the decline of serfdom in these regions and the fact that the commodity owners who did business with each other on the market were generally free and enjoyed more or less equal rights.

It is precisely this relative liberty and equality of the commodity owners within a society based on petty commodity production which allows us to grasp the real function of exchange, of the so-called 'market economy': to allow the continuity of all essential productive activities, in spite of the already well-advanced division of labour, without these activities depending on the deliberate decisions of the collectivity or of its masters.

At this stage a more or less 'anarchic' and 'free' division of labour takes over from the organisation of labour based on the deliberate and planned allocation of the work-force between the various branches of activity essential to the satisfaction of the recognised needs of the society. Chance now apparently governs the allocation of living labour and 'dead' productive resources (instruments of labour). Exchange and its results now take over from the customary or conscious planning of the allocation of these resources. But this must function in such a way as to assure the continuity of economic life (in which, it is true, many 'accidents', crises, interruptions of reproduction, and other manifestations of discontinuity occur), so that people continue to carry out all essential activities.

3 *The law of value*

It is the way in which exchange is governed that assures this result, at least in the medium and long term. Commodities are exchanged according to the quantities of labour necessary to produce them. The products of a farmer's day's work are exchanged for the products of a weaver's day's work. It is precisely at the dawning of petty commodity production, while the division of labour between the artisan and the peasant remains rudimentary, while many artisan-type activities are still performed on the farm, that it is evident that exchange can only be based on such an equivalence. Otherwise one or another of these productive activities, being less well compensated than the others, would be quickly abandoned. Thus scarcity would develop in this field. This scarcity would make prices rise, and therefore the compensation obtained by the said producers would also rise.

Then the productive efforts would be reoriented between the different sectors of activity, re-establishing the *rule of equivalence*: for the same amount of work done, the same amount of value given in exchange.

We call the law which governs the exchange of commodities and, through this, the distribution of the work-force and all the productive forces throughout the different branches of activity the 'law of value'. This is therefore an economic law essentially based on a specific form of organisation of labour, on the relations formed between human beings which are distinct from those which prevail in the organisation of an economy planned according to the customs or conscious choices of the associated producers.

The law of value assures the social recognition of labour which has become private labour. In this sense, it must function according to objective criteria which are equal for all. It is, therefore, inconceivable that a lazy shoe-maker needing two days of labour to produce a pair of shoes that a skilful shoemaker could produce in one day of labour could produce twice as much value as the latter. If the market functioned like that, compensating laziness or lack of skill, this would lead a society based on the division of labour and private labour into rapid regression and even total decline.

That is why the equivalence of days of labour which is assured by the law of value is an equivalence of labour of *socially average productivity*. In a pre-capitalist society this average is usually stable and known to all, as in such a society productive techniques develop very slowly, if at all. We can say, therefore, that *the value of commodities is determined by the quantity of labour socially necessary to produce them.*

4 The appearance of capital

In petty commodity production the small farmers and artisans go to the market with the products of their labour. These they sell in order to buy the products they need for immediate consumption but do not produce themselves. Their economic activity on the market can be summed up in the formula: *to sell in order to buy.*

However, petty commodity production very quickly necessitates a *universally accepted means of exchange* (also called a 'universal equivalent') to facilitate exchange. This means of exchange against which all commodities are exchanged independently of each other is money. With the appearance of money, another social type, another social class, can appear following the new progress in the social division of labour: the *money-owner*, separate from and opposed to the owner of simple commodities. This is the usurer or merchant specialising in international commerce.

This money-owner carries out a completely different activity on the market from that of the small peasant or artisan. As he arrives at the market with a certain sum of money, he no longer sells in order to buy, but on the contrary buys in order to sell. The small artisan or peasant sells in order to buy a commodity different from the one they produce themselves; but the aim of this operation is still the satisfaction of more or less immediate needs. On the other hand, the money-owner cannot *'buy in order to sell'* just to satisfy his needs. For the banker or merchant the phrase 'to buy in order to sell' only means something if he sells for a sum which exceeds that in his possession when he came to the market. The activity of the usurer or the merchant is therefore to increase the value of money by *surplus value, to acquire wealth as an end in itself.*

Capital — and this is what we are talking about, in its initial and elementary form: money-capital — is therefore any value which is increased by surplus value, which attempts to acquire surplus value. This Marxist definition of capital is opposed to the current definition of bourgeois manuals, according to which capital is quite simply any instrument of labour or, vaguer still, 'any durable goods'. According to this definition, the first monkey to hit a banana tree with a stick to bring a banana down would have been the first capitalist....

Let us underline it once again: like all 'economic categories', the category 'capital' can only be understood if we understand that it is based on specific *social relations between human beings*, relations which *allow* an owner of *capital to appropriate a surplus value* produced by others.

5 *From capital to capitalism*

The existence of capital is not to be confused with the existence of the capitalist mode of production. On the contrary, capital existed and circulated for thousands of years before the birth of the capitalist mode of production in Western Europe in the Fifteenth and Sixteenth Centuries.

The usurer and the merchant first appear in *pre-capitalist*, slave and feudal societies, as well as those based on the Asiatic mode of production. In these societies they operate essentially outside the sphere of production. They assure the introduction of money into a natural economy (in general this money comes from foreign parts), bring in luxury products from afar, and assure minimum credit to the possessing classes — which own much real estate but little money — as well as to kings and emperors.

Such capital is politically weak, unprotected from exactions, pillage and confiscation. That is its usual fate, and that is why its owner jealously protects his treasure, even hiding part of it, and taking care to split it up into various fields of investment for fear of provoking confiscation. Some of the richest groups of capital owners in the first centuries of the Middle Ages suffered such confiscations: for example, the Fourteenth Century Templars of France. The Italian bankers who financed the wars of the English kings in the Fourteenth Century found themselves dispossessed because these kings did not repay their debts.

It is only when the political balance of forces has changed to such an extent that these direct and indirect confiscations become more and more difficult that capital can be accumulated — can grow — in a more continuous manner. From this moment *the penetration of capital into the sphere of production* becomes possible, as does the birth of the capitalist mode of production, the birth of modern capitalism.

Now the owner of capital is no longer simply a usurer, a banker or a merchant. He is the owner of the means of production, he hires workers, and organises manufacturing and industrial production. Surplus value is no longer extracted through the sphere of distribution. It is generally *produced* during the productive process itself.

6 What is surplus value?

In pre-capitalist society, when the owners of capital essentially operate in the sphere of circulation, they can only appropriate surplus value by parasitically exploiting the revenues of other classes in society. The origin of this parasitic surplus value can be either a part of the agricultural surplus (for example, of the feudal rent) of which the nobility or the clergy are the initial owners, or a part of the slender revenues of the artisans and peasants. This surplus value is to a large extent the product of deception and pillage. Piracy, pillage and the slave-trade played an essential role in establishing the initial fortunes of the Arab, Italian, French, Flemish, German and English merchants in the Middle Ages. Later on, the purchase of merchandise at a price below its value on faraway markets, and its sale at a price higher than this value on the markets of the Mediterranean, West Europe and Central Europe, played a similar role in enriching Portuguese, Spanish, Dutch, British and French merchants and bankers.

It is clear that such surplus value as this simply results from the transfer of value. The global wealth of the society taken as a whole is scarcely increased; some lose what others gain. In fact, the global personal wealth of humanity increased by relatively little for thousands of years. It has been totally different since the arrival of the capitalist mode of production. From this moment on, surplus value is no longer simply syphoned off during the process of the circulation of commodities. It now habitually appears during the course of production itself, and therefore constantly increases in size.

We have seen that in all pre-capitalist class societies the producers (slaves, serfs, peasants) were obliged to divide their week's work, or their annual production, into a part they themselves consumed (necessary product) and a part which was appropriated by the ruling class (social surplus product). In the capitalist factory the same phenomenon occurs, although veiled by the appearance of market relations which seem to govern the 'free buying and selling' of labour power between the capitalist and the worker.

From the beginning of their day's (or week's) work in the factory, the workers incorporate a new value into the raw materials they work with. After a certain number of hours (or days) of work, they have produced a value which is exactly equivalent to their daily (or weekly) wages. If they stopped work at this precise moment, the capitalist would not obtain a penny of surplus value. But in those conditions the capitalist would not serve his own interests by buying the labour power. Like the usurer or the merchant in the Middle Ages, he 'buys in order to sell'. He buys the labour power only so that, as a result of its use, what is produced can be sold for more than what its components, including labour power, cost him to buy. This 'supplement' is his surplus value, his profit. It is therefore understood that if the workers produce the equivalent of their wages in four hours of work, they will work not four but six, seven, eight or nine hours. During these two, three, four or five 'supplementary' hours they produce surplus value for the capitalist and *gain nothing* in return.

The essence of surplus value is therefore surplus labour, 'free' labour appropriated by the capitalist. 'But it's stealing', you will say. The reply will be: 'yes and no'. Yes from the worker's point of view, no from the capitalist's point of view.

The capitalist has not in fact bought 'the value produced by, or to be produced by, the worker' on the market. He has not bought their 'labour', i.e. the labour the worker will carry out (if he had done this it would be a straightforward case of stealing — he would have paid £100 for something worth £200). He has bought the worker's *labour power*. This labour power, under capitalism, has become a commodity, and therefore has its own value as every commodity has. The value of labour power is determined by the quantity of labour necessary to reproduce it, that is necessary for the subsistence (in the larger sense of the word) of the worker and the worker's household.

Surplus value originates from the fact that a difference appears between the value produced by the worker and the value of the commodities needed to assure that worker's subsistence. This difference is due to a growth in the productivity of the worker's labour. The capitalist can appropriate to himself the advantages of that growth in the productivity of labour *because labour power has become a commodity*, because *the workers have been placed in conditions such that they no longer have access to their own means of production or of livelihood.*

7 The conditions for the appearance of modern capitalism

Modern capitalism is the product of three basic economic and social transformations:

(a) The separation of the producers from their means of production and subsistence. This separation took place in agriculture through the expulsion of small peasants from the seigneurial lands which were transformed into pastures; amongst the artisans by the destruction of the medieval corporations; by the private appropriation of the reserves of virgin lands overseas; by the private appropriation of the communally owned land in the village; etc.

(b) The formation of a social class which monopolises these means of production: the modern bourgeoisie. The appearance of this class presupposes first of all an accumulation of capital in money form, and then a transformation of the means of production which makes them so expensive that only the owners of considerable money-capital can acquire them. The industrial revolution of the Eighteenth Century, which based all future production on *mechanisation*, brought about this transformation in a definitive manner.

(c) The transformation of labour power into a commodity. This transformation results from the appearance of a class which owns nothing but its labour power, and which is obliged to sell this labour power to the owners of the means of production in order to subsist.

'Poor and needy people, of whom many are charged with the burden of women and many children, and who possess nothing other than what they can earn through the work of their hands': this excellent description of the modern proletariat is an extract from a late Sixteenth Century petition, drawn up in Leiden (in the Netherlands).

Because this proletarian mass does not have the freedom of

choice — except the choice between selling its labour power and living in permanent starvation — it is *obliged* to accept the price dictated by the normal capitalist conditions of the 'labour market' as the price for its labour power — that is to say, a sum of money just sufficient to buy commodities satisfying only those 'basic needs' which are recognised socially. *The proletariat is the class of those who are obliged by this economic constraint to sell their labour power in a more or less continuous fashion.*

1 The specific features of the capitalist economy

The capitalist economy functions according to a series of characteristics which are peculiar to it. Amongst these we will mention the following:

(a) Production essentially consists of *commodity production* — that is, production destined for sale on the market. If the commodities produced are not sold above a given price, the capitalist firms and the bourgeois class as a whole cannot get their hands on the surplus value produced by the workers and contained in the value of the commodities which have been made.

(b) Production is carried out in conditions where *the means of production are privately owned*. This private ownership is not only a legal category but above all an economic one. It means that the power to dispose of the productive forces (means of production and labour power) does not belong to the collectivity but is fragmented between separate firms controlled by distinct capitalist groups (individual and family concerns, limited companies and financial groups). Decisions to invest, which to a large extent condition the economic conjuncture, are also taken in a fragmented manner, on the basis of the private and separate interests of each capitalist unit or group.

(c) Production is carried out for an unlimited market. It is regulated by the *imperatives of competition*. From the moment when production is no longer limited by custom (as in primitive communities), or by rules and regulations (as in medieval corporations), each individual capital (each private owner, each capitalist firm or group) attempts to achieve the highest turnover, to corner the biggest share of the market, without bothering about the overall results of similar decisions taken by other firms operating in the same field.

(d) The aim of capitalist production is to maximise profit. The pre-capitalist owning classes lived off the social surplus product, generally consuming it in an unproductive manner. The capitalist class also consumes unproductively part of the social surplus product, part of the profits it acquires. But it must be able to sell the commodities in order to acquire these profits. This implies that it must offer them on the market at a lower price than that of its competitors. In order to do this it must lower the production costs. The most efficient way of lowering the production costs (the cost price) is to enlarge the basis of production — in other words, to produce more, with the aid of more and more sophisticated machines. But this constantly requires larger amounts of capital. *It is therefore under the whip of competition that capitalism is obliged to seek a maximisation of profit, so as to develop productive investments to the maximum.*

(e) Thus capitalist production appears to be production not only for profit but also for *the accumulation of capital.* In fact, the logic of capitalism requires that a major part of the surplus value be productively accumulated (transformed into supplementary capital, in the form of supplementary machines and raw materials, and extra workers), and not consumed unproductively (private consumption by the bourgeoisie and its lackeys).

Production which has as its aim the accumulation of capital leads to contradictory results. On the one hand, the increasing development of mechanisation implies an *expansion of the productive forces and a rise in the productivity of labour,* creating the material foundations for the liberating of humanity from any need 'to work by the sweat of its brow'. That is the progressive historical function of capitalism. But on the other hand, the development of mechanisation (caused by the imperative need to maximise profit and constantly accumulate capital) implies a more and more brutal subordination of the worker to the machine, of the mass of workers to the 'laws of the market' which periodically deprive them of both their skills and their jobs. Therefore the *capitalist* expansion of the productive forces implies a growing *alienation of the workers* (and, in an

indirect manner, of all the citizens of bourgeois society) from
the instruments of their labour, from the products of their
work, from their working conditions, and quite simply from
their living conditions (including the conditions governing
their use of 'free time'), and from real human relations with
their fellow citizens.

2 The functioning of the capitalist economy

In order to obtain the maximum profit and develop the
accumulation of capital as far as possible, the capitalists are
forced to reduce to a minimum the part of the new value
produced by the labour force which is returned to it in the
form of wages. This new value, this 'value added' or
'national income', is in fact determined in the productive
process itself, independent of any factors on the distribution
side. It is measurable by the sum total of the labour done by
the total number of wage-earning producers. The larger the
slice represented by the real wages paid out of this cake, the
smaller is the slice left for surplus value. The more the
capitalists try to enlarge the share taken by surplus value, the
smaller the part left for wages must necessarily become.

The two essential means by which the capitalists try to
increase their part — that is, the surplus value — are:

(a) The lengthening of the working day without any
increase in the daily wage (which took place from the
Sixteenth to Nineteenth Centuries in the West, and still
continues to this day in many colonial and semi-colonial
countries); the reduction of real wages; the lowering of the
'vital minimum'. This is what Marx called the growth in
absolute surplus value.

(b) The increasing of the productivity of labour in the
consumer goods sphere (this predominates in the West from
the second half of the Nineteenth Century onwards). After a
rise in the productivity of labour in the consumer goods
industries and in agriculture, the average industrial worker
reproduces the value of a determined number of these
consumer goods in (say) three hours of labour instead of five,
so the surplus value which they create for their boss can then
increase from the product of three hours to the product of

five hours of labour, while the working day remains fixed at eight hours. This is what Marx called *relative surplus value*.

Every capitalist tries to obtain the maximum profit. But to do this they must also attempt to increase production to the maximum, and ceaselessly lower the retail and cost prices (expressed in stable monetary units). Because of this, competition operates a selection process among the capitalist firms in the medium term. Only the most productive and the most 'viable' survive. Those who sell at too high a price not only fail to achieve the 'maximum profit' but also end up with no profit at all. They go bankrupt or are absorbed by their competitors.

The competition between capitalists leads therefore to an equalisation of the rate of profit. In the end most firms have to be content with average profits, determined in the final analysis by the total mass of social capital invested and the total mass of surplus value created by all the productive wage-earners. Only those firms enjoying a large increase in productivity, or some situation of monopoly, obtain super-profits — that is, profits above this average. In general, capitalist competition prevents super-profits or monopolies from existing for an unlimited period.

It is principally the divergences from this average profit which govern investment in the capitalist mode of production. Capital leaves the sectors where profit is below average and floods into the sectors where profit is above average (for example, it flooded into the automobile industry during the 1960s and left this sector to flood into the energy industry in the 1970s). But by flooding the sectors where the rate of profit is higher than the average, capital provokes acute competition in these sectors, followed by over-production, a lowering of the retail price, and a lowering of profits, until the rate of profit is established at more or less the same level in all industries.

3 The evolution of wages

One of the characteristics of capitalism is that it transforms human labour power into a commodity. The value of the commodity labour power is determined by its costs of reproduction (the value of all commodities which must be consumed in the reconstitution of labour power). This is therefore a matter of objective fact, independent of the subjective or haphazard estimations of groups of individuals, whether they be workers or bosses.

However, the value of labour power has a specific characteristic in relation to all other commodities: as well as a fixed stable element, it includes a variable element. The stable element is the value of the commodities needed to reconstitute labour power in a *physiological sense* (allowing the worker to recuperate the calories, vitamins and capacity to release a determined amount of muscular and nervous energy, without which it would be impossible to work at the 'normal' rhythm required by the capitalist organisation of labour at any given moment). The variable element is the value of the commodities incorporated in the 'normal standard of living' at a given epoch in a given country, over and above the physiological minimum. Marx called this part of the value of labour power its 'moral and historical' element. This means that it too is not determined by chance. It is the result of a historic evolution in the *balance of forces between capital and labour*. It is at this precise point in Marxist economic analysis that the results of past and present class struggle become a co-determining factor of the capitalist economy.

The wage is the *market price* of labour power. Like all market prices it fluctuates around the value of the commodity under examination. The fluctuations in wages are mainly determined by the fluctuations in the industrial reserve army — that is, in unemployment — and this is so in a triple sense:

(a) When a capitalist country experiences permanent and large-scale unemployment (while it is industrially underdeveloped), wages are in danger of remaining constantly under or at the level of the value of labour power. This value threatens to approach the vital physiological minimum.

(b) When massive permanent unemployment declines in the long term, mainly as a result of in-depth industrialisation and mass emigration, wages can, in a period of upturn, rise above the value of labour power. In the long term, working class struggles can bring about the incorporation into this value of the equivalent of new commodities (the socially recognised vital minimum can rise in real terms, that is, can include new needs).

(c) The highs and lows in the industrial reserve army do not only depend on demographic movements (birth and death rates) and on the international movements of emigration of the proletariat. Above all they depend on *the logic of the accumulation of capital*. In fact, in the struggle to survive competition, the capitalists have to substitute machines ('dead labour') for workers. This substitution constantly throws workers out of production. Crises play the same role. On the other hand the industrial reserve army is re-absorbed in a period of upturn and 'boom', when the accumulation of capital proceeds at a feverish pace.

There is, therefore, no 'golden rule' which governs the evolution of wages. The class struggle between capital and labour determines it in part. Capital tries to bring down wages to the vital physiological minimum. Labour tries to increase the historical and moral element of wages by including more new needs in it. The degree of cohesion, organisation, solidarity, combativity and also class consciousness of the proletariat are all factors involved in the evolution of wages. But in the long term one can discern an unquestionable tendency towards the *relative pauperisation* of the working class. The *part* of the new value created by the proletariat which goes back to the workers tends to decline (this can, however, be accompanied by a rise in real wages). The gap tends to grow between, on the one hand, the new needs created by the development of the productive forces and the growth of capitalist production and, on the other hand, the capacity to satisfy these needs with the wages earned.

A clear indication of this relative pauperisation is given by the growing divergence in the long term between the growth of the productivity of labour and the growth in real wages. In the first seventy years of the Twentieth Century, the productivity of labour in the USA and West and Central Europe in industry and agriculture rose five- or six-fold. The real wages of workers have risen only two- or three-fold in the same period.

4 The laws of motion of capitalism

Because of the characteristics of its functioning, the capitalist mode of production evolves according to certain laws of motion (laws of development) which are therefore intrinsic to its nature:

(a) *The concentration and centralisation of capital* — in competition the big fish devour the little ones, large enterprises defeat smaller ones who have fewer means at their disposal and who cannot profit from the advantages of mass production, and cannot introduce the most advanced and expensive techniques. Because of this fact the average size of these big firms grows incessantly (the concentration of capital). A hundred years ago firms with 400 employees were an exception. Today there are already firms employing more than 100,000 wage-earners. At the same time, many companies destroyed by competition are absorbed by their victorious competitors (the centralisation of capital).

(b) *The progressive proletarianisation of the working population*. The centralisation of capital implies that the number of small bosses working on their own account diminishes all the time. The fraction of the working population which is obliged to sell its labour power in order to subsist grows continually. Here are the figures relative to this evolution in the USA, which confirm this tendency in a striking fashion:

Evolution of the class structure of the USA [as a percentage of the total population in work]		
	wage earners	entrepreneurs and self-employed
1880	62	36.9
1890	65	33.8
1900	67.9	30.8
1910	71.0	26.3
1920	73.9	23.5
1930	76.8	20.3
1940	78.2	18.8
1950	79.8	17.1
1960	84.2	14.0
1970	89.9	8.9

Contrary to a well-known myth, this proletarian mass, although highly stratified, is increasing rather than decreasing in its degree of homogeneity. The difference between a manual worker, a bank employee and a low-grade civil servant is less today than it was half a century or a century ago with regard to their standard of living, their willingness to join trade unions and to go on strike, and their potential for acquiring an anti-capitalist consciousness.

This progressive proletarianisation of the population under the capitalist system mainly arises from the automatic reproduction of capitalist production relations, which stems from the bourgeois division of income already mentioned above. Whether wages be high or low, they only serve to satisfy the immediate and longer term consumer needs of the proletariat, who are incapable of accumulating fortunes. Moreover, the concentration of capital means that the cost of setting up a business constantly increases, barring the immense majority of the petty bourgeoisie as well as the whole of the working class from access to the ownership of large industrial and commercial enterprises.

(c) *The growth in the organic composition of capital.* The capital of each capitalist, and therefore the capital of all capitalists, can be divided into two parts. The first serves to buy machines, buildings and raw materials. Its value remains constant throughout production; it is simply preserved by the labour power, which transmits a part of it into the value of the products being manufactured. Marx called this *constant capital.* The second part is used to buy labour power, to pay wages. Marx called this *variable capital.* It is this part alone which produces surplus value. The relation between constant and variable capital is both a *technical* relation — in order to use a set of machines in a profitable manner they must be fed a given quantity of raw materials, and must be used by a given number of workers — and a *value* relation: a certain amount spent in wages to buy the labour power of X number of workers so as to work W number of machines costing Y pounds and transforming Z pounds worth of raw materials. Marx sums up this dual relationship of constant and variable capital by the formula: *the organic composition of capital.*

With the development of industrial capitalism this relation

tends to grow — that is, a growing mass of raw materials and a growing number of machines (which also become more and more complex) are used by one (10, 100, 1,000) worker. A higher and higher tendential value spent on machines, raw materials, energy and buildings will correspond to the same mass of wages.

(d) *The tendency of the average rate of profit to decline.* This law follows logically from the preceding one. If the organic composition of capital increases, the profit will tend to decline in relation to the total capital, because only variable capital produces surplus value, produces profit.

In this context we are speaking of a *tendential* law and not of a law which is applied in such a 'linear' manner as that of the concentration of capital or the proletarianisation of the active population. In fact there are various factors which cut across this tendency, of which the most important is the raising of the rate of exploitation of the wage-earners, the raising of the rate of surplus value (the relation between the total mass of surplus value and the total mass of wages). We must note, however, that the tendential decline of the average rate of profit cannot be lastingly neutralised by the growth in the rate of surplus value. There is in fact a limit beneath which neither the real nor the relative wage can fall without calling into question the possibility or willingness of the work-force to produce, while there is no limit on the growth in the organic composition of capital (this can increase to infinity in automated enterprises).

(e) *The objective socialisation of production.* At the start of manufacturing production each enterprise was independent of other units, and established only transient relations with its suppliers and customers. As the capitalist system evolves, lasting technical and social bonds of interdependence develop between firms and industrial sectors in a growing number of countries and continents. A crisis in one sector has repercussions in all other sectors. For the first time since the origin of the human species a common economic infrastructure is created for all humanity, a basis for their solidarity in tomorrow's communist world.

5 *The inherent contradictions of the capitalist mode of production*

From these laws of motion of the capitalist system one can spotlight a series of fundamental contradictions in the mode of production in question:

(a) The contradiction between the increasingly planned and conscious organisation of production within each capitalist firm and the more and more pronounced anarchy of the whole of capitalist production, which results from the survival of private property and generalised commodity production.

(b) The contradiction between the objective socialisation of production and the maintenance of the private appropriation of the products, profits and means of production. It is precisely when the interdependence of firms, sectors, countries and continents is at its most advanced that the fact that the whole system functions on the orders and profit calculations of a handful of capitalist magnates fully reveals its economically absurd and socially abhorrent nature.

(c) The contradiction between the tendency of the capitalist system towards unlimited development of the productive forces and the narrow limits which it is obliged to impose on the individual and social consumption of the mass of workers, since the aim of production remains maximum surplus value, which must necessitate a limitation of wages.

(d) The contradiction between the enormous leap forward in science and technology — with their potential to emancipate humanity — and the harnessing of these potential productive forces to the imperatives of the sale of the capitalist's commodities and to his *enrichment*, which leads to the situation where these productive forces are periodically transformed into destructive forces (principally through economic crises, wars and the coming to power of bloody fascist dictatorships, but also as regards the menace to humanity's natural environment), thus confronting humanity with the dilemma: socialism or barbarism.

(e) The inevitable development of the class struggle between capital and labour, which periodically undermines the normal conditions of reproduction of bourgeois society. This problematic will be examined in more detail in Chapters 8, 9,

11 and 14.

6 The periodic crises of overproduction

All the inherent contradictions of the capitalist mode of production periodically blow up in crises of overproduction. The tendency to periodic crises of overproduction, to a cyclical motion in production which successively goes through stages of economic recovery, upturn, 'boom', crisis and depression, is inherent to this mode of production and to it alone. The size of these fluctuations can vary from epoch to epoch. They are inevitable in the capitalist system.

There were economic crises in pre-capitalist societies (interruptions in normal reproduction); there are in post-capitalist society as well. But in neither case is it a question of *crises of overproduction of commodities and capital,* but rather of crises of underproduction of use values. The capitalist crisis of overproduction is characterised by a decline in income, the extension of unemployment, the appearance of desperate poverty (and often famine), brought about not because physical production has declined but, on the contrary, because it has grown in an excessive manner in relation to available purchasing power. It is because products *cannot be sold* that economic activity declines, and not because there are physical scarcities.

At the basis of the periodic crises of overproduction we find the decline in the average rate of profit, the anarchy of capitalist production, and the tendency to develop production taking no account of the limits on consumption by the working masses imposed by the bourgeois mode of distribution. As a result of the decline in the rate of profit, a growing part of capital can no longer obtain sufficient profit. Investment is reduced. Unemployment grows. The sale of a growing number of goods at a loss combines with this factor to bring about a general fall in employment, income, purchasing power and economic activity as a whole.

The crisis of overproduction is both a product of these factors and at the same time puts at the disposal of the capitalist system the means partially to neutralise its effect. The crisis brings about a decline in the value of goods and the bankruptcy of many firms. Total capital is therefore reduced in value. This permits a rise in the rate of profit and the activity of accumulation. Massive unemployment means that the rate of exploitation of the work-force can increase, which leads to the same result.

The economic crisis accentuates social contradictions and can lead to an explosive social and political crisis. It indicates that the capitalist system is ready to be replaced by a more efficient and humane system, which no longer wastes human and material resources. But it does not automatically bring about disintegration of this system. It must be overthrown by the conscious action of the revolutionary class it has engendered — the working class.

7 Unification and fragmentation of the proletariat

Capitalism raises the proletariat, concentrates it in bigger and bigger enterprises, instils industrial discipline into it, and, alongside this, provokes the emergence of elementary cooperation and solidarity in the workplace. But all this is governed by the search for **maximum profit** — **for each single** capitalist firm, and for the bourgeois class as a whole. And this class is clearly aware of the fact, confirmed by the first explosion of workers' struggles, that the concentration and unification of proletarian forces represents an enormous threat to it.

That is why the development of the capitalist mode of production is accompanied by a double, contradictory movement. On the one hand, there is the historical tendency — fundamental in the long term — towards the unification and homogenisation of the proletariat, of wage earners as a whole. But on the other hand, we see repeated attempts to fragment and divide the working class — so that certain layers are made to undergo super-exploitation and particular oppression, while others are afforded a relatively privileged status. Particular ideologies — racism, sexism, chauvinism, xenophobia — serve to justify and stabilise these particular forms of super-exploitation and oppression. Arising at the heart of the first capitalist countries, they have been sharpened and transformed into an international blight by colonialism and imperialism.

The massive employment of female and child labour was

one of the preferred means used by the early industrialists to keep down wages in the first workshops and factories. At the same time the bourgeoisie, relying above all on the catholic and muslim clergy and other agencies for disseminating reactionary ideologies, fostered the idea in the working class and other working layers of the population that 'a woman's place is in the home', and that above all women should not have access to skilled jobs and professions (where they supposedly threaten to bring about a lowering of wages).

In fact women workers and employees are super-exploited in a double sense under capitalism. In the first place because they generally receive a lower income than men — either they are less skilled, or they get lower wages for equal work (which directly increases the mass of surplus-value appropriated by capital). Secondly, inasmuch as the organisation of bourgeois socio-economic life centres on the patriarchal family as the basic unit of consumption and of the physical reproduction of the labour force, women are obliged to provide unpaid labour inside this family — in the preparation of meals, heating, cleaning, washing, care and instruction of children, etc. This work is not directly a source of surplus value, since it is not incorporated in commodities. But it increases the mass of social surplus value indirectly, in the sense that it reduces the cost to the bourgeois class of reproducing the labour force. If a male worker had to buy all his meals, clothes, heating, cleaning and laundry services on the market, if he had to pay for his children to be looked after and instructed out of school hours, his average wage would obviously have to be higher than it is while he can have recourse to the unpaid labour of his companion, his daughters, his mother, etc. And the social surplus value would be reduced accordingly.

The erratic nature of capitalist production, with its sharp rises and falls in industrial production, requires an equally spasmodic periodical inflow and elimination of labour on the 'labour market'. In order to reduce the political and social cost of such upheavals, accompanied by considerable tensions and human misery, capital has an interest in 'importing' labour originating from less industrialised countries. In so doing, it calculates not only on the passivity of this 'imported' labour, resulting from a misery and under-employment much more pronounced from the start, but also on differences in its members' customs and traditions compared with the 'indigenous' working class, hoping thereby to hold back the development of a real class solidarity and unity, which would encompass all the proletarians of every country and nation.

Huge migrations have thus occurred throughout the history of the capitalist mode of production: of Irish to England and Scotland; of Poles to Germany; of Italians, North Africans, Spaniards, and Portuguese to France; of Indians to British colonies first, and then to Great Britain; of Chinese to all the Pacific regions; of Koreans to Japan; of successive waves of immigrants to North America (English, Irish, Italians, Jews, Poles, Greeks, Mexicans, Puerto Ricans, not to mention the black slaves of the Seventeenth, Eighteenth, and Nineteenth centuries), to Argentina, to Australia, etc.

Each of these massive waves of immigration was accompanied in differing degrees by similar super-exploitation and oppression. They were made to do the least attractive work. They were forced to live in the ghettos and slums. They were were forced to live in the ghettoes and slums. They were generally deprived of all teaching in their native tongue. A thousand forms of discrimination (notably in questions of civil rights, and equal political and trade union rights) were introduced to hinder their intellectual and moral development, to keep them cowed and super-exploited, and to maintain them in a state of greater 'mobility' than the indigenous and organised proletariat (including pressure on them to return to their country of origin, or their abritrary deportation at moments of economic crisis).

The ideological prejudices simultaneously fostered inside the 'indigenous' proletariat appear to justify this super-exploitation in its eyes, thus maintaining the fragmentation and division of the working class between young and old, men and women, 'natives' and immigrants, Christians and Jews, blacks and whites, Hebrews and Arabs, etc.

The proletariat can effectively struggle to emancipate itself — or fight even at the level of defending its most immediate and basic interests — only if it unites and organises itself in such a way as to assert class solidarity and the unity of *all* of the workers. That is why the struggle against all discrimination and all forms of super-exploitation suffered by women, youth, immigrants, oppressed races and nationalities, is not merely an elementary human and political duty. It also corresponds to the proletariat's obvious class interest. The systematic education of workers to persuade them to reject all the sexist, racist, chauvinist and xenophobic prejudices which help to sustain this super-exploitation and these attempts to fragment and divide the proletariat permanently is therefore a fundamental task of the workers movement.

Chapter 6
Monopoly Capitalism

The functioning of the capitalist mode of production has not remained the same since its inception. Leaving out manufacturing capitalism, which spans the Sixteenth, Seventeenth and Eighteenth Centuries, one can distinguish two phases in the history of industrial capitalism proper:
— the phase of free competition, from the Industrial Revolution (c. 1760) up until the 1880s.
— the phase of imperialism, from the 1880s to the present day.

1 From free competition to capitalist ententes

Throughout the first phase of its existence, industrial capitalism was characterised by the existence of a large number of independent enterprises in every sector of industry. None of them could dominate the market. Each one tried to lower its prices in the hope of selling its goods.

This situation was modified when capitalist concentration and centralisation in a series of industrial sectors permitted the existence of only a reduced number of enterprises, accounting for 60 to 80 per cent of production. From then on, companies could expand and try to dominate the market, to prevent a fall in the sale price by dividing the market amongst themselves according to their relative strengths at the time.

This decline in free capitalist competition was facilitated by an important technological revolution which came about at the same time: the substitution of the electric motor and the internal combustion engine for the steam engine as the principal source of energy in industry and in the main means of transport. A whole series of new industries developed — electricity, electrical goods, oil, motor vehicles, chemical industries — which needed far greater initial capital outlay than the old sectors of industry. This in turn immediately reduced the number of potential competitors.

The principal forms of agreement between capitalists are:

— the cartel and the syndicate in a particular sector of industry, in which each firm participating in the understanding retains its independence;

— the trust and the merger of companies, in which this independence is ceded to one group of directors;

— the financial group and holding company, where a small number of capitalists control many companies and several branches of industry which, in the eyes of the law, remain independent of each other.

2 The concentration of banks and finance capital

The same process of concentration and centralisation of capital that takes place in industry and transport also takes place in banking. After this evolution, a small number of giant banks dominate the financial life of capitalist countries.

The principal role of banks in the capitalist system is to grant credit to companies. When banking centralisation is very advanced, a small number of bankers have a *de facto* monopoly on the granting of credit. This means that they no longer tend to sit back passively, merely collecting the interest on the capital they have advanced while waiting for their loan to be repaid when it falls due.

In fact, the banks which give credit to companies engaged in identical or similar activities have a major interest in assuring the viability and solvency of all these companies. They want to avoid profits falling through cut-throat competition. They intervene therefore to speed up — and sometimes to impose — industrial concentration and centralisation.

In doing this they can take initiatives to promote the creation of big trusts. In the same way, they can use their monopoly of credit facilities to obtain a stake in the capital of big companies in exchange for credit. Thus *finance capital* develops, in other words, bank capital which has penetrated industry and is able to occupy a dominant position within it.

At the top of the power pyramid in the epoch of capitalism, monopolies grow from financial groups which simultaneously control banks, other financial institutions (e.g. insurance companies), big industrial and transport trusts, big chains of retail shops, etc. A handful of big capitalists, the famous '60 families' in the USA and the '200 families' in France, possess all the levers of economic power in the imperialist countries.

In Belgium about ten financial groups control the key sectors of the economy, together with a few big foreign groups.

In the USA a few giant financial groups (in particular the Morgan, Rockefeller, Du Pont, Mellon groups, the Bank of America group, etc.) dominate the whole of economic life. It is the same in Japan, where the old *zaibatsu* (trusts), supposedly dismantled after the Second World War, have been easily reconstituted. The main groups are Mitsubishi, Mitsui, Itoh, Sumitomo, Maruberi.

3 Monopoly capitalism and free competitive capitalism

The appearance of monopolies does not mean the disappearance of capitalist competition. Even less does it mean that each sector of industry is definitively dominated by a single firm. Most importantly, it means that in the monopolised sectors:

(a) competition no longer normally takes place through the lowering of prices;

(b) because of this, the big trusts obtain monopolistic *super-profits* — that is, a rate of profit superior to that of companies in the non-monopolised sectors.

Otherwise competition continues:

(a) within the non-monopolised sectors of the economy, which are numerous;

(b) between monopolies, normally by means of techniques other than the lowering of the retail price (usually by reducing the cost price, or through advertising, etc.), and occasionally by means of a 'price war', especially where the balance of forces between the trusts has been modified and it is a matter of adapting the distribution of markets to this new balance of forces;

(c) between 'national' monopolies on the world market, essentially by the 'normal' method of the 'price war'.

However, the concentration of capital can advance to a point where, even on the world market, some firms are the last to survive in an industrial field, which can lead to the creation of *international cartels* which share out these markets.

4 The export of capital

The monopolies can only control the monopolised markets by limiting the growth of production in them, and therefore the accumulation of capital. But, on the other hand, these same monopolies are in possession of abundant capital, due mainly to the monopolistic super-profits which they have realised. The imperialist epoch of capitalism is therefore characterised by the phenomenon of surplus capital, in the hands of the monopolies of the imperialist countries, which seeks new fields of investment. The export of capital thus becomes an essential trait of the imperialist era.

This capital is exported to countries where it can reap a profit higher than the average in the competitive sectors of the imperialist countries, and can stimulate activities complementary to those of the metropolis. It is used above all to develop the production of mineral and vegetable raw materials in under-developed countries (Asia, Africa, Latin America).

As long as capitalism operated on the world market merely in order to sell its goods and buy raw materials and foodstuffs, there was no major interest in the conquest of new territories by military force (force was however used to overcome the barriers to the penetration of goods — for instance, the Opium Wars of Great Britain, carried out to force the Chinese Empire to lift the sanctions against the importing of opium from British India). But this situation was modified once the export of capital began to occupy a predominant place in the international operations of capital.

While a commodity sold is usually paid for in a few months at most, capital invested in a country is only recovered after many years. The imperialist powers therefore acquire a major interest in the establishment of permanent control over the countries in which they have invested this capital. This control is indirect in semi-colonial countries — through governments under a foreign thumb, while the state remains formally independent. In colonial countries it is direct — through an administration directly dependent on the metropolitan power. The imperialist era is therefore marked by a tendency to divide up the world into colonial empires and zones of influence of the great imperialist powers.

This division was carried out in a given period (especially between 1880-1905) as a function of the conjunctural balance of forces: the hegemony of Great Britain; the strength and importance of the French, Dutch and Belgian imperialists; the relative weakness of the 'young' imperialist powers: Germany, the USA, Italy, Japan.

A series of imperialist wars were the means by which the 'young' imperialist powers tried to use the change in the balance of forces to modify this distribution of the world in their favour: the American-Spanish war, the Russian-Japanese war, the First World War, the Second World War.

These were wars for pillage, for new fields of capital investment, for sources of raw materials, for control of markets, and not wars for a political 'ideal' (for or against democracy, for or against autocracy, for or against fascism). The same applies to the wars of colonial conquest which lie scattered through the imperialist epoch (in the Twentieth Century, the war of Italy against Turkey; the Sino-Japanese war; the Italian war against Abyssinia, in particular), or the colonialist wars against people's liberation movements (Algeria, Vietnam, etc.) in which one of the participants is there to pillage, while the semi-colonial or colonial people defend a just cause and try to escape imperialist enslavement.

5 Imperialist and dependent countries

Thus the imperialist era does not merely see the establishment of the control of a handful of financial and industrial magnates in the metropolitan countries. It is also characterised by the establishment of the control of the imperialist bourgeoisie in a handful of countries over the people of the colonial and semi-colonial countries, two thirds of the human race.

The imperialist bourgeoisie extracts considerable wealth from the colonial and semi-colonial countries. Capital invested in these countries reaps *colonial super-profits* which are brought home to the metropolis. The world division of labour based on the exchange of metropolitan manufactured goods for raw materials from the colonies leads to *unequal exchange*, in which the poor countries exchange greater amounts of labour (which is less intensive) for smaller quantities of (more intensive) labour from the metropolitan countries. The colonial administration is paid for by the taxation of the colonised peoples (a far from negligible part of this revenue is also sent to the metropolis).

The resources extracted from the dependent countries are all at once unavailable when it comes to financing their own economic growth. Imperialism is thus *one of the principal sources of the under-development* of the southern part of the globe.

6 *The era of late capitalism*

The imperialist era can itself be divided into two phases: the era of 'classical' imperialism, which covers the period before the First World War as well as the inter-war years; and the era of late capitalism, which begins at the end of the Second World War.

In this era of late capitalism, the concentration and centralisation of capital extends more and more on an international scale. While the national monopolistic trust was the 'base unit' of the era of classical imperialism, the *multinational company* is the 'base unit' of the era of late capitalism. But, at the same time, the era of late capitalism is characterised by the acceleration of technical innovation, by the quicker depreciation of capital invested in machines, by the need for big firms to calculate and plan much more precisely their costs and investments, by the tendency towards state economic programming which is the natural result of this.

The economic intervention of the state grows because the bourgeoisie needs state aid to rescue industrial sectors which have become chronically deficient; needs state financing for new and not yet viable sectors; needs to make the state *guarantee the profits of the big monopolies*, mainly by providing them with state orders (above all, but not exclusively, in the military field), subsidies, etc.

This growing internationalisation of production on the one hand, and the growing intervention of the national state in economic life on the other, leads to a series of new contradictions in the era of late capitalism, of which the crisis of the world monetary system, fed by *permanent inflation*, is one of the principal expressions.

The era of late capitalism is also characterised by a generalised disintegration of colonial empires, the transformation of colonial countries into semi-colonial countries, a reorientation in the export of capital — which now mainly moves from one imperialist country to another, and not from the imperialist countries to the colonies — and the first steps towards industrialisation (mainly restricted to the consumer goods industries) in the semi-colonial countries. This is not only an attempt on the part of the native bourgeoisies to hold back popular movements of revolt, but also a result of the fact that the export of machines and equipment today constitutes the major part of exports from the imperialist countries themselves.

Neither the transformations which have occurred in the functioning of the capitalist economy within the imperialist countries, nor those which concern the economy of the semi-colonial countries and the functioning of the imperialist system as a whole, can leave us in any doubt about the correctness of the conclusion drawn by Lenin more than half a century ago as to the historical significance of the imperialist epoch. It is the epoch of the heightening of all inter-imperialist contradictions. It is an epoch of violent conflicts, imperialist wars, wars of national liberation, civil wars. It is the epoch of revolutions and counter-revolutions, of more and more explosive confrontations, and not an epoch of gradual and peaceful progress for civilisation.

It is extremely important to do away with the myth that the present Western economy is no longer a real capitalist economy. The 1974-75 generalised recession of the international capitalist economy dealt a death blow to the theory which says that we are living in a so-called 'mixed economy', in which the regulation of economic life by the state guarantees uninterrupted economic growth, full employment, and a high standard of living for all. Reality has once again shown that the requirements of private profit continue to dominate the economy, periodically provoking massive unemployment and overproduction, and that we are still living in a capitalist economy.

It is the same with the theory which says that it is no longer the most powerful capitalist groups but managers, bureaucrats and even technocrats and academics who run Western society. This theory is not based on any serious scientific proof. Many of these alleged 'masters' of society have found themselves out on the streets during the two recent recessions. The delegation of power which big capital accepts and perfects in the giant companies it controls covers most of its traditional prerogatives except the most essential: the final decisions on the forms and fundamental direction of the accumulation and investment of capital. Safeguarded is everything to do with the 'holy of holies': the priority of the monopolies' profits, to which the distribution of dividends to shareholders can be sacrificed. Those who see this as proof that private property no longer counts for very much are forgetting the predominant tendency from the beginning of capitalism to sacrifice the private property of many little fish to that of a handful of big fish.

Chapter 7

The World Imperialist System

1 Capitalist industrialisation and the law of combined and uneven development

Modern industrial capitalism was born in Great Britain. During the Nineteenth Century it spread progressively to most West and Central European countries, as well as to the United States, and later to Japan. The existence of some already industrialised countries did not seem to prevent the successive penetration and extension of industrial capitalism into a series of countries in the process of industrialisation.

It is true that the pre-industrial forms of production in the latter (craft workers and cottage industry) were pitilessly destroyed by the cheap products of British, Belgian and French industry. But British, Belgian and French capital still had ample fields of investment open to them in their own countries. Therefore it was generally a modern national industry which increasingly substituted itself for the artisans ruined by the competition of the cheap foreign goods. In particular, this was the case with textile production in Germany, Italy, Japan, Spain, Austria, Bohemia, Czarist Russia (including Poland) and the Netherlands, etc.

This situation changed completely with the coming of the era of imperialism and monopoly capitalism. Thenceforth the functioning of the world capitalist market no longer facilitated but on the contrary held back 'normal' capitalist development, and in particular the thoroughgoing industrialisation of the under-developed countries. Marx's formula, according to which each advanced country provides a less developed country with the image of its own future, lost the validity which it had held throughout the era of free competitive capitalism.

Three essential factors (and many supplementary factors not mentioned here) determined this fundamental change in the functioning of the international capitalist economy:

(a) The volume of the mass production of many products by the imperialist countries meant that they secured such an advantage in productivity and retail price over the initial industrial production in the under-developed countries that the latter could no longer take off on a large scale, could no longer seriously sustain competition with foreign products. Increasingly it was Western industry (and later Japanese as well) which would thenceforth profit from the progressive ruin of the artisans, of cottage industry, and of manufacturing in the countries of Eastern Europe, Latin America, Asia and Africa.

(b) The surplus of capital, now more or less permanent in the industrialised capitalist countries and progressively under the control of the monopolies, unleashed a vast movement to export capital to the under-developed countries, developing areas of production there which are *complementary and not competitive* in relation to Western industry. Thus it is the domination of foreign capital over the economy of these countries which makes them specialise in the production of foodstuffs. Moreover, as these countries assume bit by bit the standing of colonial or semi-colonial countries, the state defends above all the interests of foreign capital. It does not, therefore, take even modest measures to protect emerging industries against the competition of imported goods.

(c) The domination of the economies of dependent countries by foreign capital creates an economic and social situation in which the state maintains and consolidates the interests of the old ruling classes, linking them to those of imperialist capital, rather than eliminating them radically as was the case with the great bourgeois-democratic revolutions in Western Europe and the United States.

This new evolution of the international capitalist economy in the imperialist epoch can be summed up in the law of combined and uneven development. In the backward countries — or at least in most of them — the social and economic structure is not, in its fundamental features, that of a typical feudal society nor that of a typical capitalist society. Under the impact of the domination of imperialist capital it *combines* feudal, semi-feudal, semi-capitalist and capitalist features in an exceptional manner.

The dominant social force is that of capital — but this is normally foreign capital. The native bourgeoisie does not, therefore, exercise political power. The population is not mainly composed of wage-earners, nor in most cases of serfs, but of peasants subjected in varying degrees to the exactions of semi-feudal, semi-capitalist landowners, usurers, merchants, and tax-collectors. Although living to a certain extent away from commercial production and even from monetary production, this great mass still suffers the disastrous effects of fluctuations in the price of raw materials on the world imperialist market, through the intermediary of the global effects that these fluctuations exercise on the national economy.

2 The exploitation of colonial and semi-colonial countries by imperialist capital

During successive decades the pouring of foreign capital into dependent, colonial or semi-colonial countries led to the pillage, exploitation and oppression of more than one thousand million human beings by imperialist capital. This represents one of the principal crimes for which the capitalist system has been responsible throughout its history. If, as Marx said, capitalism appeared on earth dripping blood and sweat from all its pores, nowhere is this definition justified so literally as in the dependent countries.

The imperialist epoch is above all characterised by *colonial conquest*. Colonialism does, of course, pre-date imperialism. The Spanish and Portuguese *conquistadores* had already burnt their bloody way across the Canary Isles and Cape Verde islands, as well as the countries of Central and South America, exterminating everywhere a large part, if not all, of the native population. The white colons hardly behaved in a more humane manner towards the Indians of North America. The conquest of the Indian Empire by Great Britain was accompanied by a whole host of atrocities, as was that of Algeria by France. The horrors of the slave-trade and the large-scale use of slavery in the Americas were one of the main sources of the primitive accumulation of capital.

With the arrival of the imperialist era these atrocities

extended to a great part of Africa, Asia and Oceania. Large scale massacres, deportations, expulsions of peasants from their lands, the introduction of forced labour, if not *de facto* slavery, all took place one after another. Racism 'justifies' these inhuman practices by affirming the superiority and the 'historic civilising mission' of the white race. This same racism subtly deprives the colonised peoples of their own past, at the same time as snatching away their national wealth and a large part of the fruits of their labour.

If the colonial slaves dare to rebel against their deprivation they are repressed with unspeakable cruelty. Indian women and children massacred in the Indian wars in the United States; 'mutinous' Hindus placed in front of firing cannons; tribes in the Middle East pitilessly bombarded by the RAF; tens of thousands of Algerian civilians massacred 'in retaliation' for the national insurrection of May 1945: all this foreshadows or else faithfully repeats the most savage cruelties of Nazism, including pure and simple genocide. If the European and American bourgeoisie were so up-in-arms about Hitler, it was because he committed this outrage against the white race, subjecting the peoples of Europe to that which the peoples of Asia, America and Africa had suffered at the hands of world imperialism for several centuries.

Every part of the economy of the dependent countries is subordinated to the interests and *dictates* of foreign capital. In many of these countries the railways link the centres of export production to the ports but do not link the principal urban centres to each other. The secure infrastructure is that serving the import-export activities; in contrast, the school, hospital and cultural systems are appallingly under-developed. The majority of the population languishes in illiteracy, ignorance and poverty.

Of course, the penetration of foreign capital also allows a certain development of the productive forces, gives birth to a few large industrial towns, develops a more or less important proletarian embryo in the ports, the mines, the plantations, the railways and public administration. But one can say without exaggeration that, during the three-quarters of a century between the start of the movement towards the colonisation of the entire under-developed world and the victory of the Chinese revolution, the standard of living of the average population of Asia, Africa and Latin America (apart from a few privileged countries) has stagnated or fallen. It has even fallen catastrophically in some important countries. Periodic famines have swept away literally tens of millions of Indians and Chinese.

3 The 'bloc of classes' in power in semi-colonial countries

In order to understand more completely the way in which imperialist domination has 'frozen' the development of the colonial and semi-colonial countries and has prevented normal development of the Western capitalist type, one has to understand the nature of the 'bloc of social classes' which was in power in these countries during the era of 'classical' imperialism, and the consequences of this 'bloc' on economic and social evolution.

When foreign capital penetrates massively into the colonial and semi-colonial countries, the local ruling class is generally composed of landowners (semi-feudal and semi-capitalist, in varying proportions according to the country under examination) allied to merchant and banking or usurer's capital. In the most backward countries, such as those of black Africa, it usually encounters tribal societies, in process of decomposition brought about by the prolonged effects of the slave-trade.

Foreign capital generally allies itself to these ruling classes, using them as intermediaries in the exploitation of the indigenous peasants and workers, and consolidating their relations of exploitation with their own peoples. Sometimes it even substantially extends the degree of the pre-capitalist form of exploitation, at the same time combining it with the introduction of new forms of capitalist exploitation. British colonialism transformed the *zamindari* in Bengal, who were once just tax-collectors in the service of the Mogul emperors, into straightforward proprietors of the lands from which they extracted the taxes.

Thus three hybrid social classes appear in the society of under-developed countries, setting their seal on the blocking of economic and social development:

The *compradore bourgeoisie*, a native bourgeoisie, at first simply the appointed agents of the foreign import-export houses, who acquire wealth and slowly become independent businessmen. But their businesses are essentially confined the commercial sphere (and 'services'). Their profits are usually invested in commerce, usury, the acquisition of land, and real estate speculation.

The *class of merchants and usurers*. The slow penetration of money economy dislocates the self-help mechanisms within the village community. Social differentiation pitilessly progresses in the village with the succession of good and bad harvests, on fertile and less fertile lands. Rich and poor peasants separate into two camps, with the latter depending more and more on the former. When the harvest is not sufficient to provide for even their most elementary needs, the poor peasants are obliged to take on debts in order to buy seeds and necessities. They become dependent on the merchant-money lenders, rich peasants, who, little by little, expropriate their fields and subject them to innumerable exactions.

The *rural semi-proletariat* (later extended to the urban 'fringes'). The ruined peasants who have been evicted from their lands find no work in industry, given its under-development. They are obliged to remain in the countryside and have to hire out their labour to the big peasants, or rent patches of land to scrape out a miserable existence for a ground rent (or, in the share-cropping system, in exchange for part of the harvest). This rent becomes more and more exorbitant. The more severe their misery and their lack of employment, the higher the rent they are prepared to pay for the lease of a field. The higher the ground rent is, the less it is in the interests of the owners of capital to invest in industry. Instead they use their capital to buy land. The greater the poverty of the mass of peasants, the more restricted is the interior market in consumer goods, which in turn retards industrialisation. And the more backward industry's development, the higher the level of under-development.

Under-development is not, therefore, the result of an absolute lack of capital or of resources. On the contrary, in the backward countries the social surplus product often represents a higher percentage of the national income than in the industrialised countries. Under-development is the result of a social and economic structure flowing from imperialist domination, which means that the accumulation of money capital is not principally directed towards industrialisation or even towards productive investment, which in turn leads to an immense under-employment (both quantitative and qualitative) in relation to the imperialist countries.

4 The national liberation movement

In the long term it was inevitable that hundreds of millions of human beings would not passively submit to a system of exploitation and oppression imposed upon them by a handful of big capitalists in the imperialist countries, together with the administrative and repressive apparatus at their disposal. A national liberation movement progressively takes root in the young *intelligentsia* of the Latin American, Asian and African countries. They take up the bourgeois-democratic and even socialist or semi-socialist ideas of the West in order to challenge the foreign domination of their countries. The *nationalism* of the dependent countries, which has an anti-imperialist orientation, expresses the different interests of three social forces:

— Above all, it is taken up by the *young industrial, national bourgeoisie* wherever they already possess a real material base which allows their interests to compete with those of the predominant imperialist power. The most typical case is that of the *Indian Congress Party*, led by Gandhi and heavily supported by the large Indian industrial groups.

— Due to the influence of the Russian Revolution it can be taken up by the emerging workers movement, which will use it above all as an instrument to mobilise the urban and village masses against the established power. The most typical examples are that of the Chinese Communist Party from the 1920s, and that of the Indochinese Communist Party in the following decades.

— It can promote the *explosion of revolts by the urban petty bourgeoisie and especially the peasantry,* taking the political form of *nationalist populism.* The Mexican revolution of 1910 is the best example of this form of anti-imperialist movement.

In general terms, the growing crisis of the imperialist system, marked by successive internal upheavals — the defeat of Czarist Russia in the 1904-5 war against Japan; the 1905 Russian Revolution; the First World War; the 1917 Russian Revolution; the arrival on the scene of the Indian and Chinese mass movements; the 1929-32 economic crisis; the Second World War; the defeats suffered by Western imperialism at the hands of Japanese imperialism in 1941-42; the defeat of Japanese imperialism in 1945 — forcefully stimulated the national liberation movement in the dependent countries. It received its major boost from the victory of the Chinese revolution in 1949.

The tactical and strategic problems for the international workers movement (and the indigenous mass movement in the dependent countries) which flow from the appearance of national liberation movements in the colonial and semi-colonial countries are treated in more detail in Chapter 11, point 4, and Chapter 13, point 4. Let us just underline here the particular duty of the workers movement in the imperialist countries to give unconditional support to every movement and every effective mass action in the colonial and semi-colonial countries against the exploitation and oppression to which they are subjected by the imperialist powers. This duty includes that of clearly distinguishing between inter-imperialist wars — reactionary wars — and wars of national liberation which, independent of the political force which leads the oppressed people at any particular stage of the struggle, are just wars, in which the world proletariat should work for the victory of the oppressed peoples.

5 Neo-colonialism

The upsurge of the national liberation movement in the aftermath of the Second World War led imperialism to modify its forms of domination in the backward countries. Direct domination gave way to indirect domination. The number of colonies in the true sense of the word, directly administered by the colonial power, has fallen sharply. In the space of two decades their number has fallen from about 70 to a final handful. The Italian, Dutch, British, French, Belgian and finally Portuguese and Spanish colonial empires have almost entirely collapsed.

Of course, the disappearance of the colonial empires was not unaccompanied by the counter-revolutionary resistance of important sectors of imperialist capital: the bloody colonial wars led by Dutch imperialism in Indonesia, by British imperialism in Malaysia and Kenya, by French imperialism in Algeria and Indochina, as well as the shorter but no less bloody 'expeditions' such as the Suez expedition against Egypt in 1956. But, historically, these sinister undertakings appear as rear-guard actions. Direct colonialism lies well and truly condemned.

Its disappearance in no way implies the disintegration of the world imperialist system. This continues to exist, though in modified forms. The great majority of semi-colonial countries remain confined to the export of raw materials. They continue to suffer all the unfavourable consequences of unequal, exploitative exchange. The gap between their degree of development and that of the imperialist countries continues to increase, and not to decrease. The difference between the *per capita* income and the level of well-being of the population in the 'northern' and 'southern' parts of the globe is even greater now than it was in the past.

However, the transformation from direct to indirect imperialist domination in the under-developed countries implies a stronger identification of the 'national' industrial bourgeoisie with the exploitation of the working masses of these countries, as well as a certain acceleration of the process of industrialisation. This flows both from the changed balance of political forces (that is, it represents an inevitable concession by the system to the growing pressure of the masses), and from a modification of the fundamental interests of the principal imperialist groups themselves.

There has in fact been an important alteration in the type of exports from the imperialist countries. The 'machines, equipment and transport goods' category now occupies the dominant position which used to be taken up by 'consumer goods and steel'. It is, of course, impossible for the principal monopolistic trusts to export more and more machines to the dependent countries without stimulating certain forms of industrialisation there (in general, this is restricted to the consumer goods industry).

Moreover, within the context of their world strategy, the multinational companies have an interest in implanting themselves in a certain number of dependent countries so that, given the future expansion of sales that they foresee, they are in there right from the start. Thus the practice of *joint ventures* between imperialist capital, 'national' industrial capital, private capital, and state capital is generalised in these countries. This is characteristic of the neo-colonial structure. Because of this fact, the weight of the working class in the society grows.

This structure remains within a restricting and exploitative imperialist context. Industrialisation remains limited, and its 'home market' rarely exceeds 20-25 per cent of the population — the well-to-do classes, the new middle classes, and the rich peasantry. The poverty of the masses is just as great as before. The social contradictions increase rather than diminish — from this comes the continuing potential for successive revolutionary explosions in these countries.

In these conditions a new social layer takes on importance: the state bureaucracy, which usually controls an important nationalised sector, and sets itself up as representing national interests to foreign nations while in fact profiting from its leadership monopoly to indulge in large scale private accumulation. A new 'ruling power bloc' emerges, allying foreign monopolies, 'national' industrialists and this state bureaucracy (often represented by the army). The weight of the classical oligarchy of landowners and 'compradores' declines.

Chapter 8
The Origins of the Modern Labour Movement

For as long as there have been wage-earners — in other words, long before the formation of modern capitalism — there have bẹen instances of class struggle between employers and workers. This is not the result of subversive activities on the part of individuals who 'advocate class struggle'. On the contrary, *the doctrine of class struggle is the product of the praxis of the class struggle which precedes it.*

1 The elementary class struggle of the proletariat

The first stirrings of the class struggle of the wage-earners always centre on three demands:

(1) The raising of wages, an immediate means of redistributing the social product between employers and workers in favour of the wage-earners.

(2) The reduction of working hours without loss of pay, another direct means of altering the balance in favour of the workers.

(3) Freedom to organise. While the employer, owner of capital and the means of production, has all the economic power on his side, the workers are disarmed as long as they continue to compete amongst themselves to get jobs. In these conditions the 'rules of the game' work solely to the benefit of the capitalists, who can fix wages as low as they want while the workers are obliged to accept them for fear of losing their jobs and, therefore, their means of survival.

It is by putting an end to the competition which divides them and confronting the employers *en bloc*, by refusing to work in conditions they consider unacceptable, that the workers have the opportunity to win advantages in the struggle against the capitalists. Experience rapidly teaches them that if they have not got the freedom to organise they have no weapon with which to oppose capitalist pressure.

The elementary class struggle of the proletariat has traditionally taken the form of a collective refusal to work — that is, the strike. Chroniclers have provided accounts of strikes in ancient Egypt and China. We also have the account of strikes in Egypt under the Roman Empire, especially in the First Century A.D.

2 The elementary class consciousness of the proletariat

The organisation of a strike always implies a certain — elementary — degree of class organisation. In particular, it implies the idea that the well-being of each wage-earner depends on *collective action*; it opposes a solution of *class solidarity* to an individual solution (attempting to increase individual gain without regard for the income of other wage-earners).

This idea is the elementary form of proletarian class consciousness. In the same way, in organising a strike, the wage-earners learn instinctively that they must set up relief funds. These relief funds and self-help schemes also help to diminish the insecurity of working class existence a little, and allow the proletariat to defend itself during periods of unemployment, etc. These are the elementary forms of class organisation.

But these elementary forms of consciousness and workers organisation do not imply either a consciousness of the historic goals of the workers movement or an understanding of the need for *the independent political action* of the working class.

The first forms of working class political action emerged from *the extreme left of petty-bourgeois radicalism*. In the French Revolution, Gracchus Babeuf's Conspiracy of the Equals sprang up at the extreme left of the Jacobins. This represented the first modern political movement which envisaged collective ownership of the means of production.

At the same time in England, workers set up the London Corresponding Society which tried to organise a movement of solidarity with the French Revolution. This organisation was crushed by police repression. But immediately after the end of the Napoleonic wars, a League for Universal Suffrage was created out of the extreme left of petty-bourgeois radicalism. This was essentially composed of workers from the industrial region of Manchester and Liverpool. The separation of an independent workers movement from the petty-bourgeois radical movement was accelerated after the bloody incidents of the Peterloo Massacre in 1819, and this enabled the Chartist movement to be formed a little later, as the first essentially workers organisation to demand universal suffrage.

3 Utopian socialism

All these elementary movements of the working class were largely led by the workers themselves; that is, by self-taught men who often formulated naive ideas on historical, economic and social subjects which cannot be properly explored without solid scientific studies. These movements therefore develop somewhat on the margins of the scientific progress of the Seventeenth and Eighteenth Centuries.

It is, on the contrary, within the framework of this scientific progress that the efforts of the first great utopian authors — Thomas More (Chancellor of England in the Sixteenth Century), Campanella (Seventeenth Century Italian author), Robert Owen, Charles Fourier and Saint-Simon (Eighteenth and Nineteenth Century authors) — are to be found. These authors attempt to assemble all the scientific knowledge of their epoch to formulate:

(a) a virulent critique of social inequality, especially that which characterises bourgeois society (Owen, Fourier, Saint-Simon);

(b) a plan for the organisation of an egalitarian society, based on collective ownership.

Through these two aspects of their work, the great utopian socialists are the true precursors of modern socialism. But the weakness of their system lies in the following:

(a) The society of which they dream is presented as an ideal to be constructed and achieved at one go through the understanding and the good will of men (from this comes the term — utopian socialism). It thus bears no relation to the historically determined evolution of capitalist society itself.

(b) Their explanation of the conditions in which social inequality appeared, and in which it could disappear, are scientifically insufficient and based on secondary factors (violence, morality, money, psychology, ignorance, etc.) without starting from the problems of economic and social *structure*, of interactions between the relations of production and the level of development of the productive forces.

4 The birth of Marxist theory — The Communist Manifesto

It is precisely in these two areas that the formulation of Marxist theory by Karl Marx and Frederick Engels in *The German Ideology* (1845) and especially in *The Communist Manifesto* (1847) constitutes a decisive step forward. With Marxist theory, working class consciousness is united with scientific theory at the highest level. Marx and Engels did not discover the ideas of social class and class struggle. These ideas were known to utopian socialists and bourgeois authors such as the French historians Thierry and Guizot. But they explained scientifically *the origin* of classes, the *causes* for the development of classes, the fact that the whole of human history can be *explained* by class struggle, and, above all, the *material and intellectual conditions* under which the division of society into classes can make way for a socialist, classless society.

They also explained how the development of capitalism prepares the coming of a socialist society, prepares the material and social forces which can assure the triumph of the new society. This no longer appears as a simple product of the dreams and desires of men, but as the logical product of the evolution of human history, an outcome of the actual ongoing class struggle.

The Communist Manifesto therefore represents a superior form of proletarian class consciousness. It teaches the working class that the socialist society will be the product of its class struggle against the bourgeoisie. It teaches it the necessity of struggling not simply for the raising of wages, but also for the abolition of the wages system itself. Above all, it teaches it the need to construct *independent workers parties*, and to consummate its action around economic demands through political action on a national and international scale.

The modern labour movement is therefore born of the fusion between the elementary class struggle of the working class and proletarian class consciousness brought to its highest form in Marxist theory.

5 The First International

This fusion is the end product of the whole evolution of the international workers movement between the 1850s and 1880s.

Except in Germany (with the small Association of Communists led by Marx) the working class did not appear during the European revolutions of 1848 as a political party in the modern sense of the word. Everywhere it was dragged along in the wake of petty-bourgeois radicalism. In France, it separated itself from this during the bloody days of June 1848 without, however, being able to constitute an independent political party (the revolutionary groups constituted by Auguste Blanqui were in a way the nucleus of one). After the years of reaction which followed the defeat of the 1848 revolution, it was mainly trade union and mutual aid organisations of the working class which developed in most countries, with the exception of Germany, where the agitation for universal suffrage enabled Lassalle to constitute a workers political party: the General Association of German Workers.

It was through the founding of the First International in 1864 that Marx and his little group of followers really fused with the elementary workers movement of the epoch, and prepared the establishment of socialist parties in most European countries. However paradoxical it may seem, it was not national workers parties that assembled together to constitute the First International. It was the constitution of the First International that allowed the grouping on a national level of local and syndicalist groups adhering to the First International.

When the International broke up after the defeat of the Paris Commune, the vanguard workers remained conscious of the need for organisation on a national level. After a few early defeats, the socialist parties based on the elementary workers movement of the period were definitively constituted in the 1870s and '80s. The only important exceptions were Great Britain and the USA, where the socialist parties at this time remained marginal to the already strong trade union movement. In Great Britain it was only in the Twentieth Century that the Labour Party, based on the trade unions, was created as a mass party. In the USA the creation of such a party is still today the burning task of the workers movement.

6 The different forms of organisation of the labour movement

We can thus say more exactly that the unions, mutual aid societies and socialist parties appear to a certain extent as spontaneous and inevitable products of the class struggle within capitalist society, and that which form develops first depends on factors of tradition and national particularity.

The co-operatives, however, were not the spontaneous product of class struggle, but the product of the initiative taken by Robert Owen and his comrades when they founded the first co-operative in Rochdale, England, in 1844.

The importance of the co-operative movement was real, not simply because it could provide a school for the working class in the running of the economy, but also because it could prepare the solution of one of the most difficult problems of socialist society — that of distribution — from within capitalist society. But at the same time it contained the potential danger of deviation towards economic competition with capitalist firms within the capitalist system, competition which can only have disastrous results for the working class and above all sap the class consciousness of the proletariat.

7 The Paris Commune

The Paris Commune brought together all the tendencies present in the origins and initial growth of the modern labour movement. It was born out of spontaneous mass movements and not from a plan or programme elaborated in advance by a workers party. It showed the tendency of the working class to go beyond the purely economic stage of its struggle — the immediate origin of the Commune is eminently political: the Paris workers' distrust of the bourgeoisie, who were accused of wanting to hand the city over to the Prussian armies which were besieging it — while constantly combining economic and political demands. For the first time the working class was drawn towards the conquest of political power, even at the level of just one city. The Paris Commune reflected the tendency of the working class to destroy the bourgeois state apparatus, to substitute proletarian democracy for bourgeois democracy, as a higher form of democracy. It also showed that, without a conscious revolutionary leadership, the enormous heroism of which the proletariat is capable during a revolutionary struggle remains insufficient to assure it victory.

Chapter 9
Reforms and Revolution

The birth and development of the modern labour movement within capitalist society offers us an example of the reciprocal effect between *the social milieu* in which people find themselves, independent of their wishes, and the *more or less conscious action* they develop to transform it.

1 Evolution and revolution in history

The modifications of the social system that have occurred through the ages have always been the result of sudden and violent change following wars, revolutions or a combination of the two. There is no state in existence today which is not the product of such revolutionary upheavals. The American state was born out of the 1776 revolution and the civil war of 1861-65; the British state out of the 1649 and 1688 revolutions; the French state out of the 1789, 1830, 1848 and 1870 revolutions; the Belgian state out of the 1830 revolution; the Dutch state out of the revolt of the Netherlands in the Sixteenth Century; the German state out of the 1870-71, 1914-18, 1939-45 wars, and the revolutions of 1848 and 1918, etc.

But it would be wrong to suppose that the use of violence is sufficient to change the social structure in the way desired by the combatants. For a *revolution* really to transform society and the conditions of existence of the working classes, it must necessarily be *preceded by an evolution* that creates, within the old society, the *material* (economic, technical, etc.) and *human bases* (social classes possessing certain specific characteristics) of the new society. When these bases are lacking, even the most violent revolutions end by more or less reproducing the conditions which they aimed to abolish.

A classical example of this point are the victorious peasant uprisings throughout Chinese history. Each uprising represents popular reaction against the insupportable exactions and taxes imposed on the peasants by successive declining dynasties in the 'Celestial Empire'. They lead to the overthrow of one dynasty and the coming to power of a new dynasty, often, as in the case of the Han dynasty, drawn from the leaders of the peasant insurrection themselves.

The new dynasty at first establishes better conditions for the peasantry. But the more it consolidates its power, and the more the administration entrenches itself, the more state spending increases and brings with it the obligation to raise taxes. The mandarin-functionaries, at first paid by the state treasury, begin to abuse their power and appropriate property on peasant lands, extracting a land rent over and above taxation.

Thus the growth of peasant misery reappears after a few decades of better conditions. The absence of a 'leap forward' in the productive forces and the development of modern industry founded on mechanisation explains this cyclical character of the social revolutions in classical China, and the impossibility for the peasants of achieving any lasting emancipation.

2 Evolution and revolution in contemporary capitalism

Contemporary capitalism is itself born of social and political revolutions: the great bourgeois revolutions of the Sixteenth to Nineteenth Centuries which gave birth to the nation states. These revolutions were made possible by a preceding evolution — the growth of the productive forces within feudal society, which then became incompatible with the maintenance of serfdom, the corporations, and the restrictions imposed on the free production and circulation of commodities.

This evolution also brought about the birth of a new social class, the modern bourgeoisie, which served its apprenticeship in political struggle in the medieval communes and through skirmishes with the absolute monarchy before advancing to the conquest of political power.

From a certain stage in its development, bourgeois society

too is characterised by an evolution which inexorably prepares a new social revolution.

On the material level, the productive forces develop to the point where they become more and more incompatible with the private ownership of the means of production and with capitalist relations of production. The development of large industry, the concentration of capital, the creation of trusts, the growing intervention of the bourgeois state to 'regulate' the capitalist economy, prepares the ground to a greater and greater extent for the socialisation (the collective appropriation) of the means of production, and for their planned management by the producers themselves.

On the human (social) level, a class is developed and strengthened which increasingly takes on the qualities necessary for the achievement of this social revolution: 'capitalism produces its own gravedigger in the proletariat'. Concentrated in large industries and cut off from the hope of individual social mobility, the proletariat acquires, through daily class struggle, the essential qualities of collective solidarity, co-operation and discipline in action which will make possible a fundamental reorganisation of all economic and social life.

The sharper the inherent contradictions of capitalism become, the more the class struggle hots up, and the more the evolution of capitalism prepares the revolution through explosions in various fields (economic, social, political, military, financial, etc.) during which the proletariat can attempt to gain political power and bring about a social revolution.

3 The evolution of the modern labour movement

However, the history of capitalism and that of the workers movement have not followed the clear linear trajectory anticipated by Marxists in the 1880s.

The internal economic and social contradictions of the imperialist countries did not worsen immediately. On the contrary, between the defeat of the Paris Commune and the outbreak of the First World War, Western Europe and the USA experienced a long period of growth of the productive forces, an uneven growth which concealed the internal contradictions which were undermining the system.

These contradictions were to erupt violently in 1914. The main precursors of this were the Russian revolution of 1905 and the general strike of Austrian workers in the same year. But the immediate experience of the workers and the workers movement in these countries was not of a deepening of the contradictions of the system. On the contrary, these experiences promoted the idea of a gradual, mainly peaceful and irreversible evolution towards socialism (the situation was different in Eastern Europe; hence illusions of this kind did not carry such weight).

It is true that the colonial super-profits accumulated by the imperialists allowed them to grant reforms to the workers of the Western countries. But other factors must also be considered in order to understand this evolution.

Massive emigration to the colonies and the growth of European exports to the rest of the world brought about the long-term decline of the 'industrial reserve army'. The balance of forces between capital and labour on the 'labour market' was therefore more favourable to the workers, which in turn created the basis for the growth of a mass trade unionism going beyond the ranks of the skilled workers. The bourgeoisie was frightened by the Paris Commune, by the violent strikes in Belgium (1886, 1893), by the apparently irresistible growth of German social democracy, and deliberately sought to pacify the masses in revolt by means of social reforms.

The practical result of this evolution was a Western labour movement which in fact contented itself with the struggle for immediately realisable reforms: wage increases, more social legislation, the expansion of democratic liberties, etc. It relegated the struggle for a social revolution to the domain of literary propaganda and the education of cadres. It ceased preparing itself consciously for this socialist revolution, believing that it was enough to strengthen the mass organisations of the proletariat so that, 'when the time came', this enormous force would automatically play a revolutionary role.

4 Reformist opportunism

But the role of the mass parties and trade unions of Western Europe went beyond a simple reflection of this temporary restriction of the class struggle to the terrain of reforms. They also became a political force which accentuated *the adaptation of the mass labour movement to the 'prosperous' capitalism* of the imperialist countries. Social democratic opportunism neglected to prepare the workers for the sudden imminent changes in the social, political and economic climate, and became an important factor in the survival of capitalism through the crisis years of 1914-1923.

Opportunism manifested itself *on a theoretical level* with the revision of Marxism officially proclaimed by Eduard Bernstein ('the movement is everything, our goal nothing'), who demanded that social democracy abandon all activity save that intended to reform the system. The 'Marxist centre' around Kautsky, while fighting revisionism, made numerous concessions to it, above all in justifying the daily practice of parties and unions which came closer and closer to revisionism.

Opportunism appeared *on the level of practice* with the acceptance of electoral coalitions with 'liberal' bourgeois parties, with the gradual acceptance of ministerial participation in coalition governments with the bourgeoisie, and with the lack of any determined struggle against colonialism and other manifestations of imperialism. Temporarily discredited by the consequences of the Russian revolution of 1905, this opportunism was above all displayed in Germany with the refusal to accept Rosa Luxemburg's proposal for the launching of mass strikes for political ends. It essentially reflected the particular interests of a reformist bureaucratic apparatus (social democratic officeholders, party and union officials who had acquired lavish privileges within bourgeois society).

The German example shows that the hold of reformist opportunism over the workers movement was not inevitable. It would have been possible to launch extra-parliamentary actions and broader and broader mass strikes during the years preceding the First World War. These actions would have prepared the working masses for the tasks of the revolutionary upsurge which coincided with the end of the war.

5 The need for a vanguard party

Experience therefore confirms the fundamental elements of the Leninist theory of the vanguard party. The working class can itself engage in vast class struggles around immediate objectives, and it is perfectly capable of reaching an elementary level of class consciousness. But it cannot spontaneously arrive at the superior forms of political class consciousness which are necessary in order to foresee the sharp turns in the objective situation and to elaborate the tasks of the labour movement which flow from these turns; which are necessary also in order to outwit all the manoeuvres of the bourgeoisie and to combat all the influences (however subtle) that bourgeois and petty-bougeois ideology can exercise over the working masses.

On the other hand, the mass movement inevitably experiences ups and downs. The broad masses do not permanently remain at a heightened level of political activity. A mass organisation which seeks to adapt itself to the average level of activity and consciousness of the masses will therefore often hold back the expansion of revolutionary activity, which is itself only possible at certain definite times.

For all these reasons the construction of a vanguard organisation of the working class, a revolutionary party, is indispensable. In normal times it remains a minority. But it maintains the continuity of the activity of its militants and their level of class consciousness. It allows the acquired experience of struggle to be preserved and diffused throughout the class. It prepares for future revolutionary struggles, and the preparation of these struggles is its essential task. Because of this fact, it greatly assists the changes in the ideas and activity of the organised workers and broad working masses which are required by the abrupt changes in the objective situation.

Of course, such vanguard parties cannot substitute themselves for the masses, trying to bring about the social revolution for them. *'The emancipation of the workers can only be brought about by the workers themselves.'* To win the majority of workers over to the programme, strategy and tactics of the revolutionary party — that is the necessary precondition for a vanguard party to play its full historic role.

To win over such a majority would normally only be possible at the 'high' points of pre-revolutionary or revolutionary crisis, themselves indicated by the outburst of powerful spontaneous mass movements. There is, therefore, no contradiction between the spontaneity of the masses and the necessity for the construction of a revolutionary vanguard organisation. The latter helps the former, prolongs it, completes it and permits it to triumph by concentrating all its energy at the decisive moment on the overthrow of the political and economic power of capital.

6 Revolutionaries and the struggle for reforms

Ultra-leftist attitudes, rejecting any struggle for reforms, have developed among a minority of the labour movement and the working class as a reaction to reformist opportunism.

For revolutionary Marxists, reformism is in no way identified with the struggle for reforms.

Reformism is the belief that capitalism can be abolished gradually through the accumulation of reforms. But it is perfectly possible to combine participation in struggles for immediate reforms with the preparation of the workers vanguard for anti-capitalist struggles of such an intensity and size that they bring about a revolutionary crisis in society.

The radical rejection of any struggle for reforms implies the passive acceptance of a deterioration in the situation of the working class until a moment when it would suddenly become capable of overthrowing the capitalist regime with one concerted attack. Such an attitude is both utopian and reactionary.

It is utopian because it forgets that the workers, increasingly divided and demoralised by their inability to defend their standard of living, employment and elementary rights, are hardly likely to be able to overcome a social class invested with the wealth and political experience of the modern bourgeoisie. It is reactionary because objectively it serves the cause of the capitalists — who have everything to gain by lowering wages, maintaining massive unemployment, suppressing the unions and the right to strike — if the workers passively allow themselves to be reduced to the state of defenceless slaves.

Revolutionary Marxists see the emancipation of the workers and the overthrow of capitalism as the final outcome of a period of increased organisational strength of the proletariat, of increased class cohesion and solidarity, of a growing confidence in its own strength. All these subjective transformations cannot result simply from propaganda or literary education. In the last analysis they can only result from success in the current class struggles, which are very often struggles for reforms.

Reformism is not automatically produced through such struggles and such successes. It results only if the workers vanguard abstains from educating the class in the necessity of overthrowing the system; if it abstains from the fight against the influence of petty-bourgeois and bourgeois ideology within the working class; if it abstains from engaging in practice in mass extra-parliamentary, anti-capitalist struggles which aim to go beyond the stage of reforms.

For the same reason, it is absolutely necessary for revolutionaries to work within the mass trade unions and fight for the consolidation and not the weakening of trade union organisations.

Of course, the trade unions are generally ill-equipped to prepare or to organise revolutionary struggles; that is not their function. But they are absolutely necessary for the day-to-day defence of the workers' interests against those of capital. The daily class struggle does not disappear even when capitalism is in decline. Without strong trade unions, grouping together an advanced fraction of the working class, the employers have every chance of winning the daily skirmishes. The doubts and loss of faith about their own strength which would follow on from such unfortunate experiences would be highly damaging to the development of a heightened class consciousness among the broad mass of the workers.

Moreover, in the epoch of contemporary capitalism, trade union activity no longer automatically confines itself to the fight for better wages and a reduction of the working day. More and more, workers find that they are faced with overall economic problems which affect their standard of living: inflation, taxation, cuts in social spending, factory closures, unemployment, speed-up, attempts by the state to limit the use of the right to strike and free collective wage bargaining, etc. Sooner or later any trade union is obliged to take a position on all these questions. It therefore becomes a school for the education of the working class on all problems, including the overall problems of capitalism and socialism. It becomes an arena where tendencies in favour of permanent class collaboration, and even the integration of the trade unions into the bourgeois state, confront class struggle tendencies which refuse to subordinate the interests of the workers to the supposed 'general interest' — which is merely the barely disguised interest of capital. As revolutionaries who are integrated in these class struggle tendencies best defend the immediate interests of the broad masses against attempts to divert the trade unions from their basic function, so they have the opportunity in these conditions to obtain a growing response among more and more workers, if they work with patience and perseverance and do not allow mass work to be monopolised by every shade of bureaucrat, reformist and right-winger.

Revolutionaries try to be the best trade unionists. They work continually to get the trade unions and their members to take up the objectives and forms of organisation of struggle which most clearly serve the immediate class interests of the workers. They never neglect the defence of these immediate interests, although at the same time they continuously develop their general propaganda for the socialist revolution, without which it is certain that no workers' victory can be consolidated, and no vital problem concerning the workers can be completely resolved.

The union bureaucracy, on the other hand, which is progressively integrated into the bourgeois state, increasingly substituting class conciliation and 'social peace' for its original task of the irreconcilable defence of its members' interests, objectively weakens the trade unions. It increasingly rides roughshod over the concerns and beliefs of its members, and tries to prevent the rank-and-file from determining union goals and strategy. The struggle for trade union democracy and for class struggle trade unionism therefore logically complement each other in our everyday struggles.

Chapter 10
Bourgeois Democracy and Proletarian Democracy

1 Political freedom and economic freedom

To many people who have not thought about this question, political freedom and economic freedom mean the same thing. This is particularly true of liberal social philosophy, which proclaims itself in favour of 'liberty' in every aspect of social life.

However, although political freedom can easily be defined in such a way that the liberty of some does not imply the enslavement of others, it is not so simple with economic freedom. A moment's reflection shows that most aspects of this 'economic freedom' actually imply inequality, the automatic exclusion of the major part of society from the possibility of enjoying this same liberty.

The freedom to buy or sell slaves implies that society is divided into two groups: the slaves and the slave-masters. The freedom to appropriate the means of production as private property implies the existence of a social class which is obliged to sell its labour power. What would the owner of a factory do if no-one was forced to work for someone else's benefit?

Applying their own logic in the era of early capitalism, the bourgeoisie defended on principle the freedom of parents to send ten-year-old children down the mines, the freedom to force workers to toil twelve or fourteen hours a day. But one freedom was obstinately refused — the freedom to form workers' associations, forbidden in France by the famous Le Chapellier law, which was adopted during the French Revolution under the pretext that it forbade all coalitions of a corporatist nature.

These apparent contradictions in bourgeois ideology disappear once all these attitudes are re-organised around one central theme: the defence of the property and interests of the capitalist class. That is the basis of all bourgeois ideology, not some intransigent defence of the 'principle' of freedom.

This is clearest when one examines the history of the right to vote. Modern parliamentarism was born as the expression of the right of the bourgeoisie to control public expenditure, which was financed by the taxes they paid. It was Charles I's attempt to levy taxation without summoning Parliament between 1629-40 which led directly to the English Civil War. It follows logically that the bourgeoisie denied the right to vote to the popular classes who paid no tax — after all, would not their 'demagogic' representatives continually vote for new expenditure, given that they were not the ones who paid for it?

What is at the bottom of bourgeois ideology is not at all the principle of equal rights for all citizens (its historical attitude towards the right to vote falls pitifully short of this principle), nor the principle of guaranteed political freedom for all, but, of course, the defence of wealth and the right to get rich through the exploitation of wage-labour.

2 The bourgeois state in the service of the class interests of capital

It was hardly very difficult to explain to workers in the Nineteenth Century that the bourgeois state was not 'neutral' in the class stuggle, that it was not an 'arbiter' between capital and labour, intended to defend the so-called 'general interest', but that it clearly represented an instrument for the defence of the interests of capital against those of labour.

Only the bourgeoisie had the right to vote. Only the bourgeoisie could freely refuse to employ the workers. As soon as the workers went on strike and collectively refused to sell their labour power on the conditions dictated by capital, the police or the army were sent in to fire on them. Justice was clearly class justice. Parliamentarians, judges, officers, colonial officials, ministers and bishops: they were all part of the same social class. They were bound together by common links — of money, interest and family. The working class was totally excluded from this nice little world.

This situation was modified once the modern labour movement began to grow, developed substantial organisational strength, and obtained universal suffrage through direct action (political strikes in Belgium, Austria, Sweden, the Netherlands, Italy, etc.). The working class found itself well represented in parliament (it also found itself obliged to pay a major part of taxation — but that is another story). Reformist workers parties participated in coalition governments with the bourgeoisie. In some cases they even started to make up governments exclusively composed of social democratic parties (Great Britain, Scandinavia).

Thenceforth, the illusion of a 'democratic' state above classes, a real 'arbiter' and 'conciliator' of class conflicts, was able to find a readier acceptance inside the working class. One of the essential functions of reformist revisionism is to sow widely such illusions. At one time this was the exclusive prerogative of social democracy. Today the Communist Parties, which follow a neo-reformist line, put about the same sort of illusions.

The real nature of even the most 'democratic' bourgeois state is, however, immediately revealed if one examines its practical functioning together with the material conditions for its functioning.

It is typical of the bourgeois state that, as the working masses gain universal suffrage and their representatives enter parliament in large numbers, *the centre of gravity of the state based on parliamentary democracy inexorably moves from parliament towards the apparatus of the permanent bourgeois state*: 'Ministers come and go, but the police remain.'

This state apparatus is in perfect harmony with the middle and big bourgeoisie because of the way it is recruited, its selectivity and career structure, and its hierarchical method of organisation. Indissoluble ideological, social and economic links tie this apparatus to the bourgeois class. All its top officials earn salaries which allow accumulation of capital (sometimes modest, but real for all that), giving these people an interest even as individuals in the defence of private property and the smooth running of the capitalist economy.

Moreover, the state founded on bourgeois parliamentarism is linked body and soul to capital *by the golden chains of financial dependence and the National Debt*. No bourgeois government can govern without constantly calling for credit — controlled by the banks, finance capital and the big bourgeoisie. Any anti-capitalist policies that are so much as sketched out by a reformist government come up immediately against financial and economic sabotage by the capitalists. The 'investment strike', the flight of capital, inflation, the black market, a decline in production, and unemployment quickly result from this counter-attack.

The whole of Twentieth Century history confirms that it is impossible to use a bourgeois parliament and a government based on capitalist property and the bourgeois state against the bourgeoisie in any significant way. Any policy which attempts to follow an effective anti-capitalist line is quickly confronted with a dilemma: either capitulate to the blackmail of the power of capital, or break the apparatus of the bourgeois state and replace capitalist property relations by the collective appropriation of the means of production.

3 The limits of bourgeois democratic freedoms

It is not by chance that the labour movement has been in the forefront of the struggle for democratic freedoms in the Nineteenth and Twentieth Centuries. By defending these freedoms, the labour movement at the same time defends the best conditions for its own advance. The working class is the most numerous class in contemporary society. The conquest of democratic freedoms allows it to organise, to gain the assurance of numbers, and to weigh ever more heavily in the balance of forces.

Moreover, the democratic freedoms gained under the capitalist system represent the best way to school the workers in the greater democracy which they will enjoy once they have overthrown the rule of capital. Trotsky rightly talks of 'pockets of proletarian democracy within bourgeois democracy' in relation to the mass organisations of the working class (the possibility of holding meetings and conferences, of organising strikes and mass demonstrations, of having their own press, schools, theatres, film clubs, etc.).

But it is precisely because democratic freedoms have such a great importance in the eyes of the workers that it is so necessary to grasp the limits of even the most advanced bourgeois parliamentary democracy.

First of all, bourgeois parliamentary democracy is *indirect democracy*, within which some thousands or tens of thousands of mandated persons (deputies, senators, mayors, local councillors, etc.) participate in the administration of the state. The vast majority of citizens are excluded from such participation. Their only power is that of putting a ballot paper in the box every four or five years.

Secondly, political equality in a bourgeois parliamentary democracy is a purely *formal*, and not a real equality. Formally, both rich and poor have the same 'right' to launch a newspaper — with running costs totalling hundreds of thousands of pounds. Formally, both rich and poor have the same 'right' to purchase air-time on the television, and thus the same 'possibility' of influencing the elector. But as the practical exercise of these rights presupposes access to powerful material resources, only the rich can fully enjoy them. The capitalists will succeed in influencing a large number of voters who are materially dependent on them, will buy newspapers, radio stations and time on television thanks to their money. The capitalists 'control' parliamentarians and governments through the weight of their capital.

Finally, even if one ignores all these characteristic limits of bourgeois parliamentary democracy, and wrongly supposes that it is perfect, the fact remains that it is only *political* democracy. For what is the use of political equality between the rich and poor — which is far from the case! — if it goes hand in hand with permanent, enormous economic and social inquality, which is growing all the time? Even if the rich and poor did have exactly the same political rights, the former would still have enormous economic and social power which the latter lack, and which inevitably subordinates the poor to the rich in everyday life, including the practical way in which political rights are applied.

4 Repression and dictatorship

The class nature of the state based on bourgeois parliamentary democracy appears most clearly if one looks at its repressive role. We all know of innumerable social conflicts where the police and military have intervened to break strike pickets, to disperse workers' demonstrations, to evacuate factories occupied by the workers, and to fire on strikers. We don't know of any cases in which the bourgeois police or army have intervened to arrest employers who were making workers redundant, have helped workers to occupy factories closed by capital, or have fired on the bourgeoisie which organises both the high cost of living and tax evasion schemes.

The apologists of bourgeois democracy would reply that the workers broke 'the law' in all the cases cited, and that they endangered the 'public order' which the repressive forces have to defend. We reply that this confirms that the 'law' is not neutral but is *bourgeois law which protects capitalist property*; that the forces of repression are at the service of this property; that they behave very differently according to whether it is the workers or the capitalists who commit formal breaches of 'the law'; and that nothing confirms better the fundamentally bourgeois character of the state.

In normal times the repressive apparatus only plays a secondary role in maintaining the capitalist system, since it is *de facto* respected in everyday life by the great majority of the working class. It is different in periods of crisis (whether the crisis be economic, social, political, military or financial), in which the capitalist system is profoundly disturbed, in which the working masses express their desire to overthrow the system, or in which the latter itself no longer manages to function normally.

Then repression comes to the forefront of the political scene. Then the fundamental nature of the bourgeois state quickly reveals itself in its naked form: *a body of armed men in the service of capital*. Thus a more general rule in the history of class societies is confirmed. The more stable the society is, the more it can afford the luxury of granting various formal freedoms to the oppressed. The more shaken and unstable by profound crises it is, the more it has to exercise political power through open violence rather than by means of eloquent speeches.

Thus, throughout the history of the Nineteenth and Twentieth Centuries, there are many experiences of the suppression of all the democratic rights of the workers by bourgeois dictatorships; military, bonapartist, and fascist ones. The fascist dictatorship is the most brutal and barbarous form of such dictatorships in the service of big capital.

Fascism not only suppresses the freedom of the revolutionary and radical organisations of the working class; it also seeks to crush all forms of collective organisation and resistance of the workers, including the trade unions and the most elementary forms of strikes. Furthermore, in *this attempt to atomise the working class*, it cannot simply rely on the traditional repressive apparatus (army, police, judges) if it is to be at all effective; it must be able to call on *private armies* emerging from another mass movement: that of the impoverished petty bourgeoisie, desperate because of the crisis and inflation, and yet alienated from the workers movement by the latter's failure to launch a bold anti-capitalist political offensive and to present a short-term credible alternative to the capitalist crisis.

The working class and its revolutionary vanguard cannot be neutral to the rise of fascism. They must defend their democratic freedoms tooth and nail. To this end they should counterpose to the rise of fascism a united front of all workers organisations, including the most reformist and most moderate ones, in order to crush this evil growth in the bud. They must create their own units of self-defence against the capitalists' armed groups, and not depend on the protection of the bourgeois state. *Workers' militias* supported by the mass of workers and uniting all the workers organisations, preventing every fascist attempt to terrorise any section of the masses, to break a single strike, or to smash any meeting of a workers organisation — that is the way to bar the road to the fascist barbarism which otherwise would lead to concentration camps, massacres and torture, to Buchenwald, Auschwitz, and the Santiago de Chile stadium. Every success in this fight also allows the working masses to pass onto the counter-offensive and, in opposing the fascist menace, to fight the capitalist system which gave birth to and suckled it.

5 Proletarian democracy

Marxists fight to substitute a workers state — the dictatorship of the proletariat and proletarian democracy — for the bourgeois state, which always remains, even in its most democratic form, the dictatorship of the bourgeoisie. And this workers state is characterised *by an extension and not a restriction of effective democratic freedoms* for the mass of working people. It is absolutely necessary to emphasise this basic principle, especially after the disastrous experience of Stalinism, which undermined the credibility of the democratic speeches of the official Communist Parties.

The workers state will be more democratic than the state founded on parliamentary democracy in that it *will extend direct democracy*. It will be a state which will begin to wither away from its birth, leaving entire areas of social activity to the self-management and the self-administration of the citizens concerned (post, telecommunications, health, education, culture, etc.). It will gather together the mass of working people in *workers' councils* which exercise power directly, abolishing the fictitious borderline between executive and legislative powers. It will eliminate careerism in public life by limiting the earnings of all officials, including the most highly placed, to the salary of the average skilled worker. It will cut across the formation of a new caste of administrators by introducing compulsory rotation as a principle in all delegation of powers.

The workers state will be more democratic than the state based on parliamentary democracy inasmuch as *it will create the material bases for the exercise of democratic freedoms by all*. The printing presses, radio and television stations, and assembly halls will all become collective property, and will be put at the disposal of any group of workers which wants to use them. The right to establish various political organisations and parties, including opposition ones; to create an opposition press, and the right of political minorities to express their views in the papers, on the radio and television

— these rights will be jealously defended by the workers' councils. The general arming of the working masses, the suppression of the regular army and the repressive apparatus, the election of judges, the hearing of all cases in public; these will be the best guarantee that no minority can assume the right to exclude any group of working people from the exercise of democratic freedoms.

Chapter 11

The First Inter-Imperialist War and the Russian Revolution

The outbreak of the First World War was the clearest sign that capitalism had entered into its period of decline. Everything that it had been able to contribute to the progress of humanity is henceforth threatened. Immense material resources are periodically destroyed: the First World War; the economic crisis of 1929-32; the Second World War; colonial wars of reconquest; numerous 'recessions'; the destruction of the ecological balance. The survival of capitalism is assured at the cost of millions of human lives. Bloody dictatorships, military and fascist, and the more widespread use of torture sweep away the gains of the great bourgeois-democratic revolutions. Humanity is faced with this dilemma: socialism or barbarism.

1 The international labour movement and the imperialist war

During the decade prior to 1914, the Socialist International and the entire international labour movement had begun to educate and mobilise the working masses against the growing threat of war. Increasing armament, the growth of 'local' conflicts, the heightening of inter-imperialist contradictions all clearly announced the imminent conflagration. The International reminded the workers of all countries that they had common interests and should stay out of the sordid quarrels among the ruling classes: quarrels about the distribution of the profits snatched from the proletarians and colonised peoples of the world.

But when the war broke out in 1914, most of the social democratic leaderships capitulated before the wave of chauvinism unleashed by the bourgeoisie. Each identified with 'its' own imperialist camp against the enemies of its own bourgeoisie. Everyone had an excuse. For the German and Austrian social democratic leaders, it was a matter of protecting their people against the barbarism of 'Czarist absolutism'. For the French, Belgian, and British social democratic leaders, the struggle against 'Prussian militarism' came before anything else.

In both camps the chauvinistic espousal of the national defence of the imperialist 'fatherland' implied the end of anti-militarist and revolutionary socialist propaganda, as well as the end of all defence of even the immediate class interests of the workers. The 'sacred union' of the workers and capitalists in the face of the 'foreign enemy' was proclaimed. But, like the war, this 'sacred union' in no way altered the capitalist exploitative nature of the economy and society; social patriotism implied the *de facto* acceptance of a worsening of the living and working conditions of the workers, and a scandalous growth in the wealth of the trusts and other profiteers of capitalist wars.

2 The imperialist war leads to the revolutionary crisis

But the contradictions of social patriotism soon erupted. The most artful reformist leaders explained that the masses themselves were in favour of the war, and that a mass workers party cannot oppose the predominant feelings of the people. But soon the predominant feelings within the masses turned into dissatisfaction, opposition to the war, and revolt. This time, however, the German social-patriot leaders Scheidemann and Noske and the French social-patriot leaders Renaudel and Jules Guesde did nothing 'to adapt to the predominant feelings within the working class'. On the contrary, they manoeuvred in every way to avoid the outbreak of strikes and mass demonstrations, entering into coalition governments with the bourgeoisie, helping it to suppress anti-militarist, strike and revolutionary propaganda, and sabotaging the development of the workers' struggles. When revolutions finally broke out, the social democratic leaders, who had given their approval to the massacre of millions of soldiers for the cause of capitalist profit, quickly rediscovered their pacifism and begged the workers not to have recourse to violence, not to provoke the spilling of blood.

At the beginning of the war, while the masses were disoriented by bourgeois propaganda and the betrayals of their own leaders, only a handful of revolutionary socialists remained faithful to proletarian internationalism, refusing to take up a common cause with their own bourgeoisie: Karl Liebknecht and Rosa Luxemburg in Germany; Monatte and Rosmer in France; Lenin, a section of the Bolsheviks, Trotsky, Martov in Russia; the SDP in the Netherlands; John MacLean in Great Britain; Eugene Debs in the USA; while in Italy, Serbia, and Bulgaria, a majority inside the social democratic parties held internationalist positions.

The Socialist International fell to bits. The internationalists regrouped, first at the Zimmerwald conference (1915) and then at Kienthal (1916). They were, however, divided into two currents: the centrists, who wanted to establish a reunited International with the social-patriots; and the revolutionaries, who looked towards the foundation of a Third International.

Lenin, who was the key figure in the Zimmerwald left, based his analyses on the certainty that the war was going to worsen all the contradictions of the imperialist system and lead to a large-scale revolutionary crisis. In this perspective, the internationalists could look forward to a spectacular reversal of the balance of forces between the extreme left and the right of the workers movement.

These predictions were to be confirmed from 1917 onwards. The Russian Revolution broke out in March 1917. In November 1918, revolution broke out in Germany and Austro-Hungary. In 1919-20 a revolutionary upsurge of huge proportions shook Italy, especially in the industrial North. The split between social-patriots and internationalists widened into a split between social democrats, refusing to break with the bourgeois state and capitalism, and communists, striving for the victory of the proletarian revolution and the establishment of Republics of Workers Councils. The former adopted a clearly counter-revolution-ary position once the masses threatened bourgeois order.

3 The February 1917 revolution in Russia

In February 1917 (March according to the Western calendar) the Czarist autocracy fell under the combined impact of hunger riots and the decomposition of the army (brought about by the growing opposition to the war among the peasantry). The failure of the Russian revolution of 1905 had resulted from the inability of the workers movement to link up with the peasant movement. Their coming together in 1917 was to be fatal for Czarism.

The working class had played the major role in the revolutionary events of February 1917. But, lacking a revolutionary leadership, it was robbed of victory. The executive power taken from Czarism was placed in the hands of a Provisional Government, a coalition of bourgeois parties like the Cadets (constitutional democrats) and moderate groups from the labour movement (Mensheviks and Socialist Revolutionaries).

The mass movement was, however, so strong that it had its own organisational structure: that of councils (soviets) of workers', soldiers' and peasants' delegates, backed up by the armed Red Guards. Thus, from February 1917, Russia experienced a *de facto dual power* regime. The Provisional Government, resting on a bourgeois state apparatus in slow decomposition, was confronted by a network of soviets progressively constructing a workers' state power.

Leon Trotsky's prediction at the end of the Russian revolution of 1905 that Russia's future revolution would see the blossoming of thousands of soviets was thus confirmed strikingly by events. The Russian and international Marxists had no alternative but to re-examine their analysis of the social nature of the Russian revolution in progress.

These Marxists had traditionally considered that the Russian revolution was going to be a bourgeois revolution. Russia being a backward country, the fundamental tasks of this revolution appeared to be similar to the great bourgeois revolutions of the Eighteenth and Nineteenth Centuries: the overthrow of absolutism, the winning of democratic liberties and a constitution; the liberation of the peasants from semi-feudal chains; the liberation of oppressed nationalities; the creation of a unified national market to assure the rapid growth of industrial capitalism, indispensable in preparing for the victory of a future socialist revolution. From this resulted a strategy based on an alliance between the liberal bourgeoisie and the workers movement, the latter having to content itself with the struggle for immediate class objectives (an eight hour day, freedom to organise and to strike, etc.), while pressing the bourgeoisie to fulfil more radically the tasks of 'its' revolution.

Lenin had already rejected this strategy in 1905. He recalled the analysis that Marx had made of the attitude of the bourgeoisie since the revolutions of 1848: once the proletariat appeared on the political scene, the bourgeoisie went over into the counter-revolutionary camp for fear of the workers' power. He did not modify the analysis of the historical tasks of the Russian revolution which had been traditionally formulated by the Russian Marxists. But from the clearly counter-revolutionary character of the bourgeoisie he concluded the impossibility of fulfilling these tasks through an alliance between the bourgeoisie and the proletariat. For this he substituted the idea of an alliance between the proletariat and the peasantry.

4 The theory of permanent revolution

But Lenin conceived of the 'democratic dictatorship of workers and peasants' as being based upon a capitalist economy and in the context of a state which would still be bourgeois.

As early as 1905-6, Trotsky pointed to the weakness of this conception: the chronic inability (admitted by Lenin after 1917) of the peasantry to constitute an *independent political force*. Throughout modern history the peasantry has, in the last analysis, always followed a bourgeois leadership or a proletarian one. With the bourgeoisie fatally sliding over into the counter-revolutionary camp, the fate of the revolution depends on the ability of the proletariat to conquer political hegemony over the peasant movement and establish an alliance between the workers and peasants under its own leadership. In other words: the Russian revolution could only triumph and fulfil its revolutionary tasks if the proletariat conquered political power and established a workers state, backed up by an alliance with the poor peasants.

The theory of permanent revolution therefore proclaims that in the imperialist epoch, because innumerable links tie the so-called 'national' or 'liberal' bourgeoisie in under-developed countries both to foreign imperialism and to the old ruling classes, the historical tasks of the bourgeois-democratic revolution (agrarian revolution, national independence, the conquest of democratic freedoms, unification of the country to allow the growth of industry) can only be realised through the establishment of the dictatorship of the proletariat, backed up by the poor peasants. Trotsky's prediction in 1906 was entirely confirmed by the course of the Russian Revolution of 1917. It has also been confirmed by the course of all the revolutions which have broken out since then in under-developed countries.

5 The October revolution, 1917

Coming back to Russia from abroad, Lenin immediately saw these immense revolutionary possibilities. With the *April Theses* he altered the direction of the Bolshevik Party along the lines of the theory of permanent revolution. They were to fight for the conquest of power by the soviets, for the establishment of the dictatorship of the proletariat. Although at first challenged by the old Bolshevik leaders (including Stalin, Kamenev and Molotov), who held to the formulas of 1905 and wished to reunite with the Mensheviks and give critical support to the Provisional Government, this position was rapidly accepted by the party as a whole, mainly under the pressure of vanguard Bolshevik workers who had instinctively adopted it even before it was consciously formulated by Lenin. Trotsky's followers fused with the Bolsheviks, who set about winning a majority among the workers.

After various skirmishes (the premature July uprisings, the unsuccessful counter-revolutionary *putsch* by Kornilov in August), this majority was won by the Bolsheviks in the soviets of the large towns as from September 1917. Henceforth the struggle for the seizure of power was on the agenda. This came about in October (November in the Western calendar) under the leadership of the Petrograd Military

Revolutionary Committee, headed by Trotsky and attached to the Petrograd Soviet.

This Soviet succeeded in securing in advance the loyalty of almost all the regiments stationed in the old Czarist capital; these refused to obey the general staff of the bourgeois army. Thus the insurrection, which coincided with the second All Russian Congress of Soviets, took place with little spilling of blood. The old state apparatus and the Provisional Government collapsed. The Second Congress of Soviets voted by a large majority for the coming to power of the workers' and peasants' soviets. Over the vast territory of a great country a state on the model of the Paris Commune had been set up for the first time — a workers state.

6 The destruction of capitalism in Russia

In his theory of permanent revolution, Trotsky had predicted that the proletariat could not content itself after the seizure of power with the fulfilment of the historical tasks of the bourgeois-democratic revolution, but would have to seize the factories, eliminate capitalist exploitation, and begin the construction of a socialist society. That is exactly what happened in Russia after October 1917. The revolution would 'grow over' from the fulfilment of bourgeois-democratic tasks into the realisation of proletarian-socialist tasks without interruption or stages. Hence the formula: permanent revolution — from the moment the proletariat seizes power.

The programme of the government which came to power at the end of the Second Congress of Soviets was, in the immediate term, limited to the establishment of workers control over production. The immediate tasks of the October revolution were considered above all to be the re-establishment of peace, the distribution of the land to the peasants, the solution of the national question, and the creation of real soviet power over the whole territory of Russia.

But the bourgeoisie inevitably applied itself to sabotaging the application of the new policies. The workers, now aware of their strength, tolerated neither the exploitation nor the sabotage of the capitalists. There was thus a very rapid passage from the establishment of workers control to the nationalisation of the banks, the big factories and the transport system. Soon all the means of production except those of the peasants and small artisans were in the hands of the people.

It was inevitable that the organisation of an economy based on the collective ownership of the means of production would come up against numerous difficulties in an extremely backward country, where capitalism had far from completed the task of creating the material foundations of socialism. The Bolsheviks were perfectly well aware of this difficulty. But they were convinced that they would not remain isolated for long. The proletarian revolution would surely break out in many industrially advanced countries, especially in Germany. The fusion of the Russian revolution, the German revolution and the Italian revolution could create an unshakeable material basis for the creation of a classless society.

History showed that these hopes were not without foundation. The revolution did break out in Germany. Italy did come near to the same situation in 1919-20. The Russian Revolution did play a key role as a detonator and model for the world socialist revolution. Those among the Russian and European social democrats who later declared that the 'dreams' of Lenin and Trotsky about world revolution had no basis in reality — that the Russian revolution was condemned to isolation, that it was utopian to start a socialist revolution in a backward country — forgot that the defeat of the revolutionary upsurge of 1919-20 in Central Europe was hardly due to the absence of struggles or revolutionary vigour in the masses, but arose mainly from the deliberately counter-revolutionary role played by international social democracy.

In this sense, Lenin and Trotsky and their comrades, in leading the first proletarian conquest of political power in any country, did the only thing that revolutionary Marxists can to change the balance of forces in favour of their class: to exploit to the full the most favourable chances that exist in a, country for overthrowing the power of capital. This in itself is not sufficient to *decide* the result of the international struggle between capital and labour. But it constitutes the most effective means of *influencing* the result of this struggle in favour of the proletariat.

Chapter 12
Stalinism

1 The defeat of the revolutionary upsurge in Europe, 1918-1923

The international revolution expected by the Russian proletariat and the Bolshevik leaders eventually broke out in 1918. Workers' and soldiers' councils were set up in Germany and Austria. In Hungary, a Soviet Republic was proclaimed in March 1919; in Bavaria, in April 1919. The workers of North Italy, at boiling point since 1919, occupied all the factories in April 1920. Strong revolutionary currents appeared in other countries such as Finland, Poland, Czechoslovakia, Yugoslavia and Bulgaria. In the Netherlands a general strike was on the agenda. In Great Britain the workers established the 'Triple Alliance' of the three biggest unions in the country, which shook the government.

But this revolutionary wave ended in defeat. The principal reasons for this defeat were the following:

— Soviet Russia was torn by civil war. The former landowners and Czarist officers (aided by Russian and foreign capitalists) tried to overthrow the first workers' and peasants' republic by force. Because of this, the Soviet power could give only a reduced amount of material and military aid to the European revolutions which also faced the imperialist armies.

— International social democracy placed itself in the counter-revolutionary camp without hesitation, attempting by all the promises and lies imaginable (in Germany in February 1919 it promised the immediate socialisation of big industry — which, of course, did not happen) to turn the workers away from the struggle for power. It showed no hesitation at all in organising counter-revolutionary violence, in particular through the *Freikorps* called in by Noske to oppose the German revolution. These *Freikorps* were the nucleus of the future Nazi bands.

— The young Communist Parties, which had founded the Third International, lacked experience and maturity, and made many 'leftist' and rightist errors.

— The bourgeoisie, frightened by the spectre of revolution, granted important economic concessions to the workers (notably the eight hour day) as well as universal suffrage in a number of countries. These had the effect of halting the revolutionary upsurge in some of these countries.

The first setbacks for the revolution culminated in the bloody defeats in Hungary, where the Soviet Republic was crushed, and in Italy, where fascism came to power in 1922. Nevertheless, in Germany the Communist Party grew progressively, gained a broader and broader mass base, and in 1922-23 set out to win over the big trade unions and the factory councils.

The year 1923 saw an exceptional revolutionary crisis in Germany: occupation of the Ruhr by the French army; galloping inflation; a victorious general strike which overthrew the Cuno government; Communist majorities won in large trade unions; the constitution of Left Socialist/ Communist coalition governments in Saxony and Thuringia. But the Communist Party, badly advised by the Communist International, failed when it came to the systematic organisation of the armed insurrection at the most favourable moment. Big capital re-established the former situation, stabilised the mark, and brought a bourgeois coalition back into power. The post-war revolutionary crisis was over.

2 The rise of the Soviet bureaucracy

Soviet Russia had victoriously concluded the civil war in 1920-21. But it came out of it exhausted. Agricultural and industrial production had fallen catastrophically. Famine crippled large areas of the country. To remedy this situation, while waiting for a resurgence in the international revolution, Lenin and Trotsky decided upon an economic retreat. Nationalised ownership of big industry, the banks and the transport system was maintained. But a free market was re-established for the agricultural surpluses remaining after a part had been given to the state in the form of taxation. Private trade, crafts and small-scale industry were re-established.

The Bolsheviks saw this as a temporary retreat, and calculated the risks mainly on the economic level: the petty bourgeoisie would be able to acquire wealth and constantly reproduce private capitalist accumulation. But the social and political consequences of the isolation of the proletarian revolution in a backward country were more serious than these economic dangers. They can be summed up like this: *the Russian proletariat progressively lost the direct exercise of political and economic power*. A new privileged layer began to emerge which acquired a real monopoly of the exercise of power in all areas of society.

This process was not the result of a premeditated plot. It resulted from the interaction of a large number of factors. The proletariat was numerically weakened by the fall in industrial production and the exodus into the countryside. It was partially depoliticised under the weight of famine and hardship. Its most conscious elements were absorbed into the Soviet apparatus. Many of its best elements were killed in the civil war. This whole troubled period was not favourable to the formation of technically and culturally qualified cadres inside the working class. Hence the petty-bourgeois and bourgeois intelligentsia retained their monopoly of knowledge. A period of great poverty favours the acquisition and defence of material privileges.

Neither should we imagine that this process passed unnoticed by the Russian revolutionary Marxists. From 1920 the Workers Opposition within the Soviet Communist Party sounded the alarm, although the solutions it proposed were largely inadequate. From 1921 Lenin was obsessed by the bureaucratic danger, calling the Russian state a *bureaucratically deformed workers state* and powerlessly recording the hold of the growing bureaucracy on the apparatus of the party itself. In 1923 the Trotskyist Left Opposition was established, making the struggle against the bureaucracy one of the key points of its programme.

It would, however, be incorrect to believe that the rise of the Soviet bureaucracy was inevitable. Although it had profound roots in the social and economic reality of Russia at the beginning of the 1920s, this does not mean that there was no real chance of opposing it successfully. The programme of the Trotskyist Left Opposition was aimed entirely at creating the favourable conditions needed to put the situation to rights:

(a) by accelerating the industrialisation of Russia, thus increasing the specific weight of the proletariat in society;

(b) by increasing wages and fighting unemployment, with a view to increasing the confidence of the working masses in themselves;

(c) by immediately increasing democracy in the soviets and in the party, with a view to raising the level of political activity and class consciousness of the proletariat;

(d) by accentuating the class differences within the peasantry: providing credit and agricultural machinery to help the poor peasants, while burdening the rich peasants with increased taxes;

(e) by continuing to look towards the world revolution, and by rectifying the tactical and strategic errors of the Comintern.

If the Bolshevik leaders and cadres as a whole had understood the necessity and possibility of achieving such a programme, the revitalisation of the soviets and the exercise of power by the proletariat would have been possible from the mid-1920s. But the majority of the cadres of the party were themselves caught up in the process of bureaucratisation. The majority of the leaders understood too late the mortal threat contained in the rise of the bureaucracy. The failure of the 'subjective factor' (of the revolutionary party), together with the necessary objective conditions, explains the victory of the Stalinist bureaucracy in the USSR.

3 *The nature of the bureaucracy: the nature of the USSR*

The bureaucracy is not a new ruling class. It plays no indispensable role in the process of production. It is a privileged layer which has usurped the exercise of administrative functions in the Soviet state and economy, and which uses this monopoly of power to grant itself big advantages as consumers (high wage differentials, fringe benefits, advantages in kind, special shops, etc.). It does not own the means of production. There is no way in which it can guarantee the maintenance of advantages, nor transmit them to its children: all this is linked to the exercise of specific functions.

It is a privileged social layer of the proletariat, whose power rests on the conquests of the October socialist revolution: nationalisation of the means of production; a planned economy; state monopoly of foreign trade. It is conservative in the same way as is every workers bureaucracy: it puts the preservation of what has been gained above the extension of the revolutionary conquests.

It is afraid of international revolution, which threatens to revive the political activity of the Soviet proletariat and thus undermine its own power. It wants to maintain the international *status quo*. But as a social layer it remains opposed to the re-establishment of capitalism in the USSR, which would destroy the very foundations of its privileges (not that this prevents the bureaucracy from spawning sub-groups and tendencies which try to transform themselves into new capitalists).

The USSR is not a socialist society — that is, a classless society. It remains just as it was immediately after the October 1917 revolution, a society in transition between capitalism and socialism. Capitalism could be restored there, but only through a *social counter-revolution*. The direct power of the workers could be restored, but only through a *political revolution* which would break the bureaucrats' monopoly over the exercise of power.

The Soviet economy cannot be given the tag of 'capitalist' because it is a system of 'domination of the producer by the bureaucrats'. Capitalism is a *specific* system of class domination, characterised by the private ownership of the means of production, competition, generalised commodity production, the transformation of labour power into a commodity, the necessity to *sell* all produced commodities before the surplus value contained in them can be realised, the inevitability of periodic crises of generalised overproduction. None of these fundamental characteristics can be found in the Soviet economy.

But if the Soviet economy is not capitalist, neither is it socialist in the traditional sense of the term employed by Marx, Engels and Lenin himself. A socialist economy is defined as the regime of *associated producers*, who themselves regulate their productive and social life by establishing a hierarchy of needs to be satisfied depending on the resources at their disposal and the amount of work they are prepared to dedicate to the productive effort. The Soviet Union is a long way from such a situation. A socialist economy is defined by the disappearance of commodity production. In contradiction to the current official doctrine of the USSR, Marx and Engels clearly state that this withering away is in no way part of the 'second phase' of classless society, commonly known as the 'communist phase', but is a characteristic of the first phase, commonly known as 'socialist'.

In developing the anti-Marxist theory of *the supposed possibility of completing the construction of socialism in one country*, Stalin expressed in a pragmatic manner the petty-bourgeois conservatism of the Soviet bureaucracy: a mixture of old officials of the bourgeois state, jumped-up elements of the Soviet state apparatus, demoralised and cynical communists, young technicians eager to 'make a career' without regard to the class interests of the proletariat as a whole.

In opposing to this theory the basic thesis of Marxism ('classless society can only be achieved on the international level, including at the very least some of the principal industrialised countries of the world' — 'the socialist revolution begins on the national arena, it unfolds on the international arena, and is completed on the world arena'), Trotsky and the Left Opposition hardly defended a 'defeatist', 'wait and see' position regarding the fate of the Russian revolution. Long before Stalin they tried to encourage the more rapid industrialisation of the country. They were, and remain, supporters of the defence of the USSR against imperialism, of the defence of what remains of the conquests of the October revolution against any attempt to restore capitalism in the USSR. But they understood that the fate of the USSR would finally be settled by the result of the class struggle at an international level. Today, as previously, this conclusion remains correct.

4 What is Stalinism?

When he pronounced his famous indictment of the crimes of Stalin at the Twentieth Congress of the Communist Party of the Soviet Union, Nikita Khrushchev explained these crimes by the 'personality cult' which had reigned during Stalin's dictatorship. This subjective, even psychological, explanation of a political regime which completely changed the lives of tens of millions of human beings is incompatible with Marxism. The phenomenon of Stalinism cannot be reduced to the psychological or political peculiarities of one man. We are dealing with a *social* phenomenon whose *social* roots must be laid bare.

In the USSR, Stalinism is the expression of the *bureaucratic degeneration* of the first workers state, where a privileged social layer usurped the exercise of political and economic power. The brutal forms (police terror; the massive purges of the '30s and '40s; the assassination of almost all the old cadres of the CPSU; the Moscow trials, etc.) as well as more 'subtle' forms of this bureaucratic power can vary. But after Stalin, as under him, the fundamental characteristics of the bureaucratic degeneration still remain.

Power is not exercised by the soviets, freely elected by all the workers. The factories are not managed by the workers. Neither the working class nor the members of the Communist Party enjoy the democratic freedoms necessary to be able to decide freely on the major questions of economic and cultural, domestic and international policy.

In the capitalist world, Stalinism signifies the subordination, by the parties which follow the Kremlin, of the interests of the socialist revolution in their own countries to the interests of Soviet diplomacy. Instead of serving as an instrument for the analysis of the evolution of the contradictions of capitalism, the relation of forces between the classes, the objective reality of the transition period between capitalism and socialism, so as to aid the struggle for the emancipation of the proletariat, Marxist theory is debased to the level of an instrument to justify each 'tactical turn' of the

Kremlin and the Stalinist parties.

Stalinism tries to justify these manoeuvres as necessary for the defence of the USSR, the 'chief bastion of the world revolution' before the Second World War, and the 'centre of the world socialist camp' since then. The workers must essentially defend the USSR against imperialism's attempts to re-establish the rule of capital there.

But the Stalinist tactical manoeuvres which have contributed to the defeat of so many revolutions in the world; which eased the coming to power of Hitler in Germany in 1933; which condemned the Spanish revolution of 1936 to defeat; which obliged the French and Italian communist masses to reconstruct the bourgeois state and the capitalist economy in 1944-46; which led to the bloody crushing of the revolutionary movement in Iraq, Indonesia, Brazil, Chile and many other countries since then; these manoeuvres hardly correspond to the interests of the Soviet Union as a state. They correspond to the narrow interests of the defence of the privileges of the Soviet bureaucracy — contrary, in all these cases, to the true interests of the USSR.

5 The crisis of Stalinism

The decline of the international revolution after 1923 and the backward state of the Soviet economy: those were the two main pillars of bureaucratic power in the USSR. But both have been gradually undermined since the end of the 1940s.

Twenty years of defeats for the revolution have been followed by a new rise in the world revolution, at first confined to equally under-developed countries (Yugoslavia, China, Vietnam, Cuba), extending into the West since May 1968. After years of effort aimed at 'socialist accumulation', the USSR has ceased to be an under-developed country. Today it is the second industrial power in the world, with a technical and cultural level as high as that of many advanced capitalist countries. The Soviet proletariat, along with that of the USA, is numerically the strongest in the world.

In these conditions, the basis for the passivity of the masses in countries dominated by the Soviet bureaucracy has begun to disappear. The beginnings of oppositional activities have been accompanied by splits within the bureaucracy itself, which has been undergoing a process of growing differentiation since the Stalin-Tito rupture in 1948. The interaction between these two factors favours a sudden eruption of political action by the masses, who have taken up the tasks of the political revolution, as in October-November 1956 in Hungary, or during the 'Prague spring' of 1968 in Czechoslovakia.

Until now these mass movements have been suppressed by the military intervention of the Soviet bureaucracy. But as the same process ripens in the USSR, no exterior force will be able to halt the tide of political revolution in Eastern Europe and the USSR. Soviet democracy will be re-established. All danger of the restoration of capitalism will disappear forever. Political power will be exercised by the workers and poor peasants. The struggle for the socialist revolution in the rest of the world will be greatly advanced.

6 Economic reforms

After Stalin's death, and above all during the '60s and '70s, a vast movement of reform in methods of planning and management has taken place in the USSR and 'People's Democracies'. The most urgent reforms took place in agriculture, where the production of foodstuffs per head of the population was lower at the time of Stalin's death than it had been in 1928, and was even lower than during the Czarist epoch in the case of livestock. Successive measures aimed to promote an increase of income for the peasants, the rationalisation of the use of agricultural machines (which were sold to the *kolkhozes*), the establishment of enormous state farms on the 'virgin lands' of Kazakhstan, and the massive growth of investment in agriculture.

The reforms in industry were both slower and more hesitant. The objective necessity for these reforms flows from the crisis of growth of the Soviet economy, from a fall in the annual growth rate of industrial production. It corresponds to the exhaustion of the reserves in productive resources which had allowed extensive industrialisation to function more or less adequately — that is, with no efforts being made to economise to the maximum on labour, raw materials and land. The exhaustion of reserves brings with it the obligation to calculate more exactly, to make more rational choices between various investment projects. The growth in the economy itself, the multiplication of enterprises and their resources, risked increasing wastage endlessly unless more rational methods of planning and management were introduced.

The pressure of the working masses, weary of decades of sacrifice and tension, and wishing to improve and diversify their level of consumption, as well as the need to bring the decisions — at the level of light industry — into line with the consumers' desires, both pointed in the same direction. Yet another element encouraged the drive for reform: a growing technological backwardness in relation to the third technological revolution of the capitalist economy, a backwardness flowing from the system of material incentives for the bureaucracy, which discourages technological experimentation and innovation. The form of these incentives was henceforth modified.

By linking the managers' bonuses to the 'profits' (the difference between the cost price and the selling price), which are said to 'synthesise' the global performance of the enterprise, rather than to gross production expressed in physical terms, the bureaucratic leaders hoped to discourage wastage of raw materials and labour and to encourage a more rational use of machinery. The results were modest but positive in light industry. But they hardly made any difference to the hybrid nature of the system, since the selling prices continued to be fixed by the authorities of the central plan.

The scope of all these reforms is limited because they do not resolve the fundamental problem. No 'economic mechanism' outside of democratic and public control by the mass of producers and consumers can achieve a maximum return for a minimum effort. Each reform tends to substitute a new form of bureaucratic abuse and wastage for the old form. No global rationalisation of planning is possible under the rule of the bureaucracy and its material privileges, which are seen as the principal motor for the realisation of the plan. The reforms have not restored capitalism, nor have they reintroduced profit as a guide for investment decisions. But they have increased the internal contradictions of the system. On the one hand they have accentuated the thrust of one faction of the bureaucracy in favour of a greater autonomy for the factory managers, threatening key gains of the working class such as the guaranteed right to work; and on the other hand they have increased the resistance of the workers to the tendencies to chip away at their gains and the planned economy.

7 Maoism

The victory of the third Chinese revolution in 1949 was the most important gain for the world revolution since the victory of the October socialist revolution. It broke the capitalist encirclement of the USSR, greatly stimulated the process of permanent revolution in Asia, Africa and Latin America, and tangibly altered the balance of forces on a world scale to the disadvantage of imperialism. This could come about because, *in practice*, the Maoist leadership of the Chinese CP had broken with the Stalinist line of the 'bloc of four classes' and revolution by stages, had led a vast peasant uprising, and had destroyed the bourgeois army and the bourgeois state, in spite of its proclamations in favour of a coalition with Chiang Kai-shek.

However, this victorious revolution was bureaucratically deformed from the outset. The independent action of the proletariat was strictly limited, if not prevented, by the Maoist leadership. The workers state which was established was in no way based on democratically elected workers' and peasants' soviets. Forms of managerial and bureaucratic privileges, imitations of those in force in Stalinist Russia, were widespread. This provoked a growing discontent among the masses, and especially among the workers and youth, which Mao tried to channel by launching the 'Great Proletarian Cultural Revolution' in 1964-5.

This combined genuine forms of anti-bureaucratic consciousness and mobilisation in the urban masses with an attempt by Mao to purge the CP apparatus and eject his opponents from the bureaucracy. When the mass mobilisations and the increasingly critical ideological evolution of the 'Red Guards' almost escaped from their control, the Maoist faction put an end to the 'Cultural Revolution'. It re-established the unity of the bureaucracy to a large extent, bringing back into leadership positions most of the bureaucrats thrown out at the height of the 'revolution'.

The Sino-Soviet conflict was provoked by the attempt of the Soviet bureaucracy to impose a monolithic control over the leadership of the Chinese CP and its move to withdraw economic and military aid to the People's Republic of China as a reprisal for Mao's refusal to give way to these *ukases*. This conflict steadily moved from being an inter-bureaucratic, organisational and ideological battle within the international Stalinist movement into one at state level. The narrow nationalism of the bureaucracy, Soviet as well as Chinese, dealt a severe blow to the interests of the world workers and anti-imperialist movement as imperialism was able to gain new room for manoeuvre by exploiting the Sino-Soviet conflict.

On the ideological level Maoism represents a current which is part of the workers movement, with aspects which are a variety of the Stalinist deformation of Marxism-Leninism. While Stalinism is at the same time the product and expression of a political counter-revolution within a victorious proletarian revolution, Maoism is the expression both of the victory of a socialist revolution and of the bureaucratically deformed nature of this revolution from its very beginning. It therefore combines characteristics of a more flexible and eclectic approach to the relations between the apparatus and the masses with the characteristic trait of smothering any independent action or organisation on the part of the masses, especially on the part of the urban proletarian masses.

In particular, it is characterised by an incomprehension of the social nature of the workers' bureaucracy, and of the origins of the possible bureaucratic degeneration of socialist revolutions and workers states — since it is itself the ideological expression of one fraction of the bureaucracy. In identifying in an irresponsible and non-scientific manner 'bureaucracy' with the 'state bourgeoisie' in the USSR, and in defining the USSR as 'social-imperialist', it justifies in advance all the turns in Chinese foreign policy and those of the Maoist groups. It even goes so far as to put American imperialism, the USSR, bourgeois parties and Communist Parties on the same footing, not to mention its designation of the USSR and the CPs as the 'principal enemy of the people', and its offers of an alliance with imperialist powers and bourgeois parties against the Soviet Union and the CPs. These 'tactics' are based on the theory according to which most of the capitalist countries are not faced today with the task of socialist revolution but with that of struggling for national independence from the two 'super-powers'.

The arbitrary character of all these theories, which are in fact just belated justifications for Peking's diplomatic manoeuvres, has its roots in a voluntarist and idealist deformation of Marxism. Under the pretext of fighting 'economism' as the 'most dangerous' revision of Marxism, the 'orthodox' Maoists cease to consider social classes as objective realities determined by the production relations in a given society. Social classes are identified with ideological options. The proletariat is no longer the total mass of wage-earners, but those who 'follow Mao Tse-tung thought'.

In this way, petty-bourgeois or bourgeois ideological currents *within the working class* are identified with 'the bourgeoisie' or 'its representatives', and the ideological struggle within the workers movement is identified with the 'class struggle between the proletariat and the bourgeoisie'. From this flows the rejection of workers democracy, the justification for using violence and repression within the workers movement, the rejection of the whole Marxist-Leninist tradition of struggling for a united front of all workers organisations against the common class enemy. The dictatorship of the proletariat is identified with 'Mao Tse-tung thought' and exercised by the 'Mao Tse-tung party'.

Thus we come full circle. After declaring war on the power of the bureaucracy in the USSR, the Maoists end up defending a regime of bureaucratic command which is very similar to that existing in the USSR, even if it is topped off with a bit of fancy icing in the form of 'participation' of the masses in decision making. Maoism does not accept the Leninist theory of the dictatorship of the proletariat, based on the exercise of power by freely and democratically elected workers' and peasants' councils, any more than Stalin, Khrushchev or Brezhnev.

Chapter 13

From the Current Mass Struggles to the World Socialist Revolution

Since the First World War, the necessary material conditions have existed for the building of a socialist society. Big factories have become the basis of production. The world division of labour has reached a high level. The interdependence of all people — the 'objective socialisation of production' — has been largely achieved. Hence it becomes objectively possible to replace the system of private property, of competition and market economy, by a system based on the association of all producers and the planning of production in order consciously to satisfy democratically determined needs.

1 The conditions for the victory of the socialist revolution

But the existence of the material conditions necessary to bring about that revolution is in and by itself not sufficient for its victory. Contrary to all the social revolutions in the past, the socialist revolution demands a *conscious and deliberate* effort on the part of the revolutionary class: the proletariat. While the revolutions of the past substituted one system of economic exploitation of the producers for another, and had to be content with trying to smooth the functioning of a particular economic mechanism, the socialist revolution seeks to organise the economy and society according to a preconceived plan: the conscious organisation of the economy in order to satisfy all the rational needs of humanity and to assure the full development of the personality of all human beings.

Such a plan will not fulfil itself automatically. It requires a clear consciousness of its aims and the means of achieving them on the part of the revolutionary class. This is especially true as, in its struggle for the socialist revolution, the working class will have to confront a class enemy which is much better organised, with a world network of military, financial, political, commercial and ideological forces at its disposal to maintain its domination.

The victory of the world socialist revolution therefore requires two sorts of conditions if it is to be successful:

— *Objective* conditions: that is, independent of the level of consciousness of the proletariat and the revolutionaries. Among these we class the maturity of the *social and material conditions* (economic basis and numerical strength of the proletariat), *permanently* achieved on a world scale before 1914. *Political conditions* also come into this classification: the inability of the bourgeois class to rule, and its growing internal divisions; the refusal of the productive classes to accept bourgeois rule and their growing rebellion against it. These objective political conditions which are necessary for the victory of a socialist revolution are met *periodically* in various countries when profound pre-revolutionary and revolutionary crises break out.

— *Subjective* conditions: that is, the level of class consciousness of the proletariat, and the degree of maturity, influence and strength of its revolutionary leadership, its revolutionary party.

One can conclude that victorious socialist revolutions have been objectively possible on numerous occasions in many countries since the First World War. Just to deal with the industrially advanced ones: in Germany in 1918-20 and 1923, and probably in 1930-32 as well; in Italy in 1919-20, in 1946-48, in 1969-70; in France in 1936, in 1944-47, in May 1968; in Great Britain in 1919-20, in 1926, in 1945; in Spain in 1936-37, etc.

On the other hand, the subjective conditions were not ripe for the victory of the revolution. The absence of revolutionary victories in the West has therefore been, until now, essentially a function of the 'crisis of the subjective factor in history', of the crisis of the class consciousness and the revolutionary leadership of the proletariat.

2 The construction of the Fourth International

It was because they started from such an analysis, based on the historic failure of reformism and Stalinism to lead the proletariat to victory, that in 1933 Trotsky and a handful of opposition communists set themselves the task of creating a new revolutionary leadership for the world proletariat. In 1938 they established the Fourth International for this purpose.

The Fourth International is not yet in itself the revolutionary mass International which alone will be capable of functioning as a real general staff of the world revolution. But it transmits, sharpens up and improves the programme of such a mass revolutionary International, thanks to its constant activities within the class struggle in sixty countries. It forms cadres on the basis of this programme, through its many activities. It thus encourages in a deliberate manner the unification of the experiences and consciousness of revolutionaries on a world scale, teaching them to act within a single world organisation instead of vainly expecting such unification to come about spontaneously through the upsurge of revolutionary forces in various countries and regions of the world, each developing in isolation from the others.

The Fourth International does not just wait passively 'for the time to come', niggling over its programme while it waits. It does not restrict itself to abstract propaganda for its programme. Neither does it waste its strength in sterile activism and agitation which is limited to support for the immediate struggles of the exploited masses.

The construction of new revolutionary parties and a new revolutionary International combines: the intransigent defence of the revolutionary Marxist programme, which brings together the lessons of all the past experiences of the class struggle; propaganda and agitation for an action programme, part of the general revolutionary Marxist programme that Trotsky called a *programme of transitional demands*, drawing on the terms used by the leaders of the Communist International during the first years of its existence; and a constant intervention in the struggles of the masses in order to bring them, through their experience, to acceptance of this action programme, and to give forms of organisation to these struggles which will teach them to create workers' councils during revolutionary crises.

The need for a revolutionary International which is more than the sum total of national revolutionary parties is based on solid material foundations. The imperialist epoch is the epoch of *world* economy, *world* politics, and *world* wars. Imperialism is a cohesive international system. The productive forces have already been internationalised for a long time. Capital is increasingly organised internationally in *multinational corporations*. The nation state has long been a hindrance to the furtherance of production and civilisation. The great problems of humanity (the prevention of nuclear world war; the elimination of hunger; the planning of economic growth; the equitable division of resources and income amongst all peoples; the protection of the environment; the utilisation of science for the people) can only be resolved on a world scale.

In these conditions, it is clearly utopian to progress towards socialism with dispersed forces, utopian to fight an enemy organised on a world scale while scorning any international co-ordination of our revolutionary project, utopian even to hope to defeat the multinational corporations through workers' struggles limited to one country.

Moreover, revolutionary struggles have an objective and spontaneous tendency to spread internationally, not only in response to the counter-revolutionary interventions of the class enemy but above all because they are a stimulant for the workers of many countries. To put off continually the creation of a real international *organisation* of revolutionaries is not just to lag behind the objective necessities of our epoch, but is also to lag behind the spontaneous tendencies of the most advanced sections of the masses themselves.

3 Immediate demands, transitional demands

In our epoch, capitalist exploitation and imperialist oppression again and again arouse the masses to major struggles. But by themselves the masses generally do not go beyond the formulation of the most immediate aims of these struggles: the defence or increase of real wages; the defence or conquest of certain fundamental democratic freedoms; the fall of particularly oppressive governments, etc.

The bourgeoisie can grant concessions to the masses in struggle to prevent these struggles from developing to the point where they threaten capitalist exploitation in its entirety. It is even more willing to do this because it possesses innumerable means of neutralising these concessions, of taking back with one hand what it has given with the other. If it accepts a rise in wages, an increase in prices can maintain profits. If working hours are reduced, the rhythm of work can be stepped up. If the workers win measures of social security, taxes can be increased so that they themselves end up paying for what the state seems to be handing out, etc.

To break this vicious circle, the masses must be won to the adoption of transitional demands as the objectives of their present struggles — demands whose realisation becomes more and more incompatible with the normal functioning of the capitalist economy and the bourgeois state. These demands need to be formulated in such a way that they can be understood by the masses — otherwise they will just remain demands on paper. At the same time, their nature should provoke, by their very content and the depth of the struggles unleashed, a challenge to the entire capitalist system and the birth of organs of self-organisation of the masses, organs of dual power. Far from being valuable only in times of acute revolutionary crisis, transitional demands — such as the demand for workers control — tend precisely to give birth to such a revolutionary crisis by encouraging the workers to challenge the capitalist system in action as well as in their consciousness.

4 The three sectors of world revolution today

Because of the delay of the socialist revolution in the industrially advanced countries, the world proletariat finds itself confronted with different tasks in different parts of the world.

In the colonial and semi-colonial countries, the workers and poor peasants cannot wait until the workers of the industrialised countries come to their aid. Given the enormous burden of oppression and misery that imperialism has imposed on the masses in those countries, the eruption of vast mass struggles and vast revolutionary movements there is inevitable. The workers must support every anti-imperialist mass movement, whether it is directed against foreign political domination or against exploitation by foreign trusts; whether it is for the peasant revolution or the elimination of bloody native dictatorships. Having won the political leadership of these mass movements through its resolve and energy in making the progressive demands of all the exploited classes and layers of the nation its own, the proletariat fights for the conquest of power, and at the same time overthrows the property and power of the native bourgeoisie. This is the strategy of permanent revolution.

In the bureaucratised workers states, the masses rise up to obtain democratic freedoms against the bureaucracy's monopoly over the exercise of power, against the reappearance of national oppression, against corruption, waste, and the material privileges which characterise the bureaucratic management of the economy. They demand the running of the workers' state by the workers themselves, organised in their councils (soviets) with a plurality of parties and full democratic rights for all, the management of the planned economy by a system of democratically centralised workers' councils. This is the strategy of the political anti-bureaucratic revolution.

In the imperialist countries, the mass movements against capitalist exploitation, against the restriction or the suppression of democratic freedoms, are transformed through the transitional programme and the construction of a new revolutionary leadership into struggles for the overthrow of the bourgeois state and the exploitation of capital, for the collective ownership of the means of production and socialist planning, into a victorious socialist revolution. This is the strategy of the social revolution of the proletariat.

The different tasks faced by the proletariat and the revolutionaries in different parts of the world — tasks of the permanent revolution in under-developed countries, tasks of the anti-bureaucratic political revolution in the bureaucratised workers states, tasks of the proletarian revolution in the imperialist countries — reflect *the unequal and combined development of the world revolution*. This revolution does not break out simultaneously in all countries. All countries are not in an identical social, economic and political condition.

The supreme task of revolutionary Marxists is the progressive unification of these three revolutionary processes into one and the same *process of world socialist revolution*. This unification is possible because only one social class, the proletariat, can successfully advance the distinct historic tasks of the revolution in each of the three sectors we have mentioned. This unification will take place thanks to the *internationalist politics and education* of the revolutionary vanguard, which will bring to the present struggles more and more experiences of the international solidarity of the workers and oppressed people of all countries, and which will fight in a systematic manner against chauvinism, racism, and nationalist prejudices of any kind in order to infuse this internationalist consciousness into broader and broader masses.

5 Workers democracy, the self-organisation of the masses and socialist revolution

One of the main aspects of the direct action of the masses, of their strikes or mass mobilisations, is the raising of their level of consciousness through the growth of their confidence in themselves.

In daily life the workers, poor peasants, small artisans, women, youth, national and racial minorities are all used to being crushed, exploited, and oppressed by a multitude of possessors and powers. They tend to feel that revolt is impossible and useless, that their enemies are too strong, that it will all end up in a 'return to order'. But in the heat of mobilisations and great mass struggles, this fear, this feeling of inferiority and powerlessness, suddenly begins to disappear. The masses become conscious of their immense potential power as soon as they act together, collectively and in solidarity, as soon as they organise themselves and organise their struggles effectively.

That is why revolutionary Marxists attach extreme

importance to everything which increases the self-confidence of the masses, everything which helps to break them from the obedient and servile behaviour which has been impressed on them through thousands of years of domination by the possessing classes. 'Servile masses, arise, arise': these words from the first verse of the 'Internationale' perfectly express the psychological revolution which is needed for the victory of the socialist revolution.

Democratic assemblies of strikers electing strike committees, and every similar mechanism in other forms of mass action, play a vital role in developing the self-organisation of the masses. In these assemblies the masses learn about self-government. In learning to conduct their own struggles, they learn to run the state and economy of tomorrow. The forms of organisation to which they become accustomed are thus the embryonic forms of the future workers' councils, the future soviets, the basic forms of organisation of the workers state to be.

The *unity of action* which is needed to bring together the scattered forces of the workers; the powerful tide of unity which, in large mobilisations and mass actions, unites millions of individuals who have not been used to acting together — this unity *cannot be achieved without practising the widest possible workers democracy*. A democratically elected strike committee must by definition be the expression of *all* the strikers in the factory, the industry, the town, region or country on strike. To exclude the representatives of any particular group of workers, on the pretext that their political or philosophical opinions don't meet with the approval of those who are temporarily leading the strike, is to break the unity of the strike and therefore to break the strike itself.

The same principle applies to all forms of mass action and to the forms of representative organisation which are thrown up in their course. The unity which is needed for victory presupposes workers democracy — that is, the principle of not excluding any current among those in struggle. Everyone should have the right to defend their particular proposals in order to make the struggle successful.

If this democracy is respected, the minorities in their turn will respect the majority decisions, because they will still have an opportunity to modify these in the light of experience. Through this affirmation of workers democracy, the democratic forms of organisation of workers' struggles also proclaim a characteristic of tomorrow's workers state: the extension and not the restriction of democratic freedoms.

Chapter 14
The Winning Over of the Masses by the Revolutionaries

1 Political differentiation within the proletariat

We have seen (Chapter 9, point 5) how the need for a revolutionary vanguard party arises from the intermittent character of the direct action of the masses, as well as from the scientific nature of the strategy needed to overthrow the power of the bourgeoisie. We can now add a further factor to this analysis — the political differentiation within the proletariat.

In every country of the world, the workers movement appears as the sum total of *different ideological currents*. Existing side by side are the social democratic current, classical reformists; the official pro-Moscow CP current, of Stalinist origin and increasingly neo-reformist in its orientation; the anarchist and anarcho-syndicalist current; the Maoist current; the revolutionary Marxist current (the Fourth International). In many countries there are also intermediary formations (centrists) in between these principal ideological currents.

This ideological differentiation in the workers movement has many objective roots in the reality and history of the proletariat.

The working class *is not entirely homogeneous* from the point of view of its social conditions of existence. Depending on whether they work in large or small scale industries, have been urbanised for several generations or very recently, are highly skilled or merely have average skills, the workers tend to grasp certain basic ideas of scientific socialism with varying degrees of rapidity.

The highly skilled groups of workers can understand the need for trade union organisation much more quickly than workers who have been unemployed for half their lives. But their trade union organisation also runs the risk of succumbing more quickly to the temptations of narrow corporatism, subordinating the general interests of the working class to the specific interest of a *working class aristocracy* which defends the specific advantages it has acquired by attempting to prevent access to the trade. It is easier for workers in large towns and industries to become conscious of the enormous potential strength of the great proletarian masses, and to grasp the possibility of a victorious proletarian struggle to seize the power and factories from the bourgeoisie, than it is for workers in small firms or those living in small towns.

Added to the non-homogeneity of the working class is the *diversity of its experience in struggle and its individual capacities*. One group of workers may have had experience of a dozen strikes (most of them successful) and many demonstrations. This experience will help to determine its consciousness in a different manner from that of another proletarian group which may have experienced only one strike (which failed) in ten years and has never participated *en bloc* in a political struggle. One worker or employee may be naturally interested in study and may read pamphlets and books as well as the newspapers. A different worker may hardly ever read. One may be combative by temperament and even be a born leader; another may be more passive and prefer to remain aloof. One may make friends easily with workmates; another may be more of a home-bird and more absorbed in domestic life. All this will partially influence the behaviour and the political choice of individual workers, and their level of class consciousness at a given moment.

Finally, we must take into account *the specific history and national traditions* of the workers movement in each country. The British working class, the first to achieve independent political class organisation with the *Chartist movement*, has never had the experience of a mass party based on Marxist education or a Marxist programme, even at an elementary level. Its mass party, the Labour Party, is based on and born out of mass trade unionism.

The French working class, heavily influenced by its own specific traditions of the first half of the Nineteenth Century

(Babeufism, Blanquism, Proudhonism), was held back in coming to Marxism by the relative weakness of large industry, and by its relative dispersal in comparatively small provincial towns. It needed the growth of large factories in Paris, Lyon, Marseilles and the North-East of France between the two World Wars, and again during the '50s and '60s, before the general course of class struggle could be determined by the mass strike (June 1936, the strikes of 1947-8, May 1968) and before the French Communist Party could become the dominant party of the working class, giving it an outlook and a tradition which have explicit reference to Marxism.

The Spanish working class and workers movement has long been marked by a revolutionary syndicalist tradition, strongly influenced by the pronounced under-development of large industry in the Iberian peninsula, etc.

The diversity of ideological currents in the workers movement is a result of its own logic and history — that is, of debates and oppositions produced by the process of class struggle itself. The First International was split between Marxists and anarchists on the question of the need to conquer political power. The Second International was split between revolutionaries and reformists on a number of questions: participation in bourgeois governments, support for national defence in the imperialist countries, support or suppression of the revolutionary struggle of the masses at the precise moment when it was threatening the survival of the capitalist economy and the bourgeois state based on parliamentary democracy. The Third International was split between Stalinists and 'Trotskyists' (revolutionary Marxists), between supporters and opponents of the theory of permanent revolution and the theory of 'revolution by stages', between supporters and opponents of the utopia of completing the construction of socialism in one country, and, from that, between supporters and opponents of the subordination of the interests of the international revolution to the alleged needs of this completion.

But even this diversity of ideological currents also has deeper objective and material roots.

2 The united working class front against the class enemy

The diversity of ideological currents within the workers movement has led to a fragmentation of the political organisations of the working class. While trade union unity exists in many countries (Great Britain, Scandinavia, the German Federal Republic, Austria), the division into different political organisations is universal. As materialists, we must understand that this is the result of objective causes and not of chance — the 'crimes' of the 'splitters' or the 'criminal role' of any individual or small group of 'traitors'.

This political division is not in itself a bad thing. The working class has been able to win some of its most startling victories in conditions where many parties and tendencies co-existed, all simultaneously proclaiming adherence to the workers movement. The Second All-Russian Congress of Soviets, which decided to transfer all power to the soviets, was marked by a deeper fragmentation into different political parties and tendencies of the working class than anything we now see in the West. The division of the German working class into three large parties (and a number of smaller groups and currents) did not prevent the victory of the general strike of March 1920, which nipped the reactionary Kapp *putsch* in the bud. The diversity of political and trade union organisations of the Spanish proletariat in July 1936 did not prevent it from responding correctly to the military-fascist uprising in almost all the industrial centres.

But the political diversity of the workers movement leaves intact the striking force of the working class as a whole only so long as it does not prevent the unity in action of the workers against the class enemy: the employers, the big bourgeoisie, the bourgeois government, the bourgeois state. A further precondition is the ability of the revolutionary Marxists to wage a political and ideological struggle for hegemony in the working class and for the construction of the revolutionary mass party — in other words, the existence of workers democracy within the organised workers movement and a correct political line put forward by the revolutionary Marxists.

The unified response of the working class is essential above all *against the offensives of the bourgeoisie*. This may be an economic offensive: redundancies, factory closures, wage cuts, etc. It may be political: attacks on the right to strike and on trade union liberties; attacks on the democratic freedoms of the masses and the workers movement; attempts to establish authoritarian or openly fascist regimes, suppressing the freedom of the workers movement as a whole. In all these cases only a massive and united response can defeat the bourgeois offensive. Real unity in action by the working class comes through a real united front of all workers organisations which retain any influence among important sections of the proletariat.

One of the greatest tragedies of the Twentieth Century was the defeat of the German proletariat by Hitler's conquest of power on 30 January 1933, as a result of the refusal and the inability of the leaderships of the KPD (German CP) and SPD (Social Democrats) to reach a united front agreement against the rise of Nazism in time. The consequences of this tragedy were so great that every worker must absorb the principal lesson of this experience: *the united front of all workers organisations is indispensable against the rise of fascism*, in order to prevent, through the united and resolute action of the working masses, the rise to power of assassins, torturers and hangmen.

The barriers and obstacles on the road to achieving the united front are essentially of a political and ideological nature: the workers in their great majority are instinctively favourable to any united initiative. Among these political and ideological obstacles we can single out:

* The repressive practices of the social democratic leaders — and of the Stalinist leaders when they also find themselves in the same position — whenever they exercise responsibility in the bourgeois state. The radicalised layers of the working class are rightly indignant at such practices, which include everything from the 'simple' act of breaking strikes to the systematic organisation of betrayals within the workers organisations, and even the organisation of the assassination of revolutionary leaders or even ordinary workers (Noske!)

* The bureaucratic and manipulative practices of the reformist and Stalinist trade union leaders, CP leaders

catapulted to leading positions in the workers movement, etc. These practices, added to the repressive practices of the bureaucracy where it is in power, also provoke justified hostility among several layers of workers.

* The systematically counter-revolutionary role of the traditional leaders of the workers movement, who undermine the growth in class consciousness, objectively (and often deliberately) aid the counter-revolutionary and anti-working class projects of big capital, spread bourgeois and petty-bourgeois ideology within the working class, etc.

Nevertheless, we must *fight sectarianism and ultra-leftism* with regard to the traditional mass organisations of the workers movement — sectarianism and ultra-leftism which are not merely obstacles on the road to achieving the united workers front against the class enemy, but also obstacles on the road to an *effective struggle* against the hold of the reformist and Stalinist leaderships over the majority of the working class.

A failure to understand the *double and contradictory nature* of the traditional and bureaucratised mass organisations of the workers movement lies at the root of these sectarian and ultra-leftist errors. (More generally, sectarianism is characterised on the level of theory by the exaggeration of one particular aspect of tactics or strategy, by the inability to see the problems of class struggle and the proletarian revolution in all their complexity, in their entirety.) It is true that the policies of the leaderships of these organisations are largely favourable to the bourgeoisie, that they practise class collaboration, weaken the class struggle of the proletariat, and are responsible for countless defeats suffered by the working class, Nevertheless, it is equally true that the existence of these organisations allows the workers to reach a minimum class consciousness and strength without which the development of this class consciousness would become much more difficult.

The existence of these organisations also allows a modification of the *daily* balance of forces between capital and labour, without which the self-confidence of the working class would be badly shaken. Only their *immediate* replacement by higher forms of class organisation (workers' councils) would prevent their weakening from being accompanied by a retreat or a paralysis of the working class. Their weakening, let alone their destruction, by capitalist reaction would represent a grave weakening and setback for the whole of the proletariat. That is the principled basis on which revolutionary Marxists fight for their policy of the workers united front against capitalist reaction.

3 The offensive dynamic of the 'class against class' front

Confronted by any capitalist offensive against the working class, especially the threat of a right-wing dictatorship or fascism, revolutionary Marxists propose the construction of a united front of all workers organisations from the rank-and-file upwards. They try to involve *all* the organisations claiming to be part of the workers movement, including the most moderate, and those with the most opportunist and revisionist leaderships. They systematically call on the leaders of the SP, the CP, the reformist and Catholic unions to join in the establishment of a united front of national, regional and local leaderships as well as those in the factories and localities, in order to face up to the enemy offensive with all appropriate means.

The refusal to pursue the united front to the leadership level in the social democratic or Communist parties (the so-called 'Third Period' politics of the Comintern, taken up today by quite a few Maoist-Stalinist organisations) is based on an ultimatist and infantile lack of understanding of the objective function of, and the subjective preconditions for, the unity of the proletarian front. It presupposes that the mass of Socialist workers (or those following the CP) are already prepared to engage in united action with revolutionary workers without the previous agreement of their 'social-fascist' or 'revisionist' leaders. It therefore treats as resolved the task that remains to be solved: that of *detaching* the masses from the opportunist leaders *through their own experience*. In fact, it is precisely the call to the SP and CP leaderships to join in a united front against the offensive of reaction which allows the workers who follow these leaderships to go through the valuable and necessary experience of judging the credibility, effectiveness and good faith of these leaders.

Furthermore, to suggest that it is not necessary to involve the SP and CP leaderships in the workers united front gives rise to the assumption that the revolutionaries are already a majority in the working class, and spreads grave illusions as to the possibility of overthrowing capitalism, the bourgeois state, or the fascist menace, through minority coups.

Is this to say that the workers united front is a tactic which is strictly limited to defensive ends? Not at all. The organisation of the entire working class into one striking force — even if at first for defensive ends — modifies the balance of forces between the classes, and considerably reinforces the militancy, strength, self-confidence and capacity for political action of the working masses. It therefore creates an immense *further potential for struggle* which can quickly turn a defensive struggle into an offensive one. At the time of the Kapp *putsch* in Germany, in March 1920, the victorious and united response of the German workers organisations created a situation in which militants from many organisations — even reformist organisations — decided within the space of a few days in several Ruhr towns to set up armed workers militias. The call for a workers government was even advanced by the most moderate trade union leaders. The victorious and united response of the Spanish masses in most large towns to the fascist *putsch* of July 1936 led to the general arming of the proletariat and the seizure of the factories.

In order to exploit fully the offensive potential of the workers united front, revolutionary Marxists put forward the need to *structure* the united front at the base as well as the top, without turning this call into an ultimatum to the workers parties, trade unions or masses. This proposal implies that, apart from national and regional agreements and 'blocs' of workers organisations, the united front should involve *local committees*, in factories, estates and localities — committees which must evolve as quickly as possible into *democratically elected* committees engaged in systematic mobilisations and mass actions. The offensive dynamic of such a structure is evident, as it would clearly open up a revolutionary situation.

4 The workers united front and the popular front

Just as revolutionary Marxists are the strongest supporters of the workers united front, so they reject the politics of the 'Popular Front' — a revival, dating from the Seventh Congress of the Comintern, of the old reformist social democratic policy of an alliance between the 'liberal' (or 'national' or 'anti-fascist') bourgeoisie and the workers movement ('left bloc').

There is a fundamental difference between the workers united front and the 'left bloc' or 'Popular Front'. Through its 'class against class' logic, the workers united front unleashes a dynamic which develops and sharpens the struggle of the proletariat against the bourgeoisie. The Popular Front, on the contrary, through its collaborationist logic, unleashes a dynamic which holds back the workers' struggles and even represses the most radicalised layers of workers. While the workers united front against the capitalist offensive contains no preconditions about the defence of bourgeois order and capitalist property (no matter how much the reformist leaders are attached to this defence), the Popular Front is explicitly based on the respect of bourgeois order and property — without which, they say, the presence of the 'progressive bourgeoisie' within the front would be impossible; and this, in turn, would 'reinforce reaction'. The whole logic of the Popular Front therefore tends to deflect, contain or break mass struggles, which is not the case with the workers united front.

Of course, while the distinction between the workers united front and the Popular Front is considerable because of the objective class nature of the two types of agreement, there is no 'absolute' difference. There could be opportunist applications of the united front tactic in which the leaders of self-styled revolutionary organisations began themselves to hold back the mass struggle under the pretext that you must not 'frighten the reformist leaderships'. On the other hand, Popular Front agreements in certain situations can lead the masses away from collaborationist illusions and towards an increase of their struggles and even to the creation of structures of self-organisation — initiatives which revolutionary Marxists must, of course, support and back up in every way possible.

But regardless of such intermediary situations, the question of principle remains vital. From the point of view of the class struggle, we must support workers united front policies; we must fight any political pact with bourgeois parties, even 'left-wing ones', which would challenge the political class independence of the proletariat.

5 Political class independence and united class organisation

Thus, like the Popular Front problematic, the united front problematic leads on to one vital question: how can the working class achieve the united organisation of its strength, in total independence from the bourgeoisie, in spite of its fragmentation into ideological currents and different political parties, groups and sects, and in spite of the insufficient average level of class consciousness?

Those who put forward the disappearance of this fragmentation as a *prior condition* for the achievement of united class organisation live in the land of make-believe. This fragmentation has existed for a century. There is no indication that it will easily disappear. To consider its disappearance in this way is effectively to say that the unity of the proletarian front (and therefore its victory) is a possibility lost in the mists of time.

Those who see the achievement of the unity in action of the class simply as a result of top-level agreements, independent of the class content and objective dynamic unleashed by these agreements — those, for example, who positively identify the united front with the Popular Front — forget that the real unity of the proletarian front is only possible on a class basis; it is, in fact, unthinkable that all the sectors and layers of the working class could accept the self-limitation and self-mutilation contained in class collaborationist agreements.

There is, therefore, a close link between the unity in action of the working class as a whole and the common acceptance of its aims of struggle, and even the forms of struggle adopted by the class. Revolutionary Marxists are totally in favour of any unifying initiative because they are convinced that such initiatives always reinforce the militancy and consciousness of the workers towards an unyielding class struggle against capital.

The class independence of the proletariat, without which its unity cannot be achieved, applies in relation to the employers at the level of the factory and industrial sector; in relation to the bourgeois parties; and in relation also to the bourgeois state, even the freest, most bourgeois-democratic state. The self-confidence gained by the working class through the experience of real, class-wide unity drives it to take the solution of all problems into its own hands, even those problems normally left to parliament. This is another reason why revolutionaries are the most resolute and consistent advocates of the unity in action of the entire working class.

6 Class independence and alliances between the classes
The distinction in principle which we are making here between the workers united front and the Popular Front has often been criticised as 'dogmatic'. It 'tries to deny the need for alliances'. Without 'alliances between classes' the victory of socialist revolution would be impossible. Did not Lenin base the whole Bolshevik strategy on the need for an alliance between the proletariat and the peasantry?

Let us say first of all that any parallel between the imperialist countries of today and Czarist Russia is misguided. In Russia the proletariat represented 20 per cent of the active population. In the imperialist countries, with the exception of Portugal, the proletariat — that is, the mass of those who are obliged to sell their labour power — represents the overwhelming majority of the nation, 70-80 per cent of the active population in most of these countries. The unity of the proletarian front (including white collar workers, of course) is infinitely more vital for the revolution than an alliance with the peasantry.

Let us add that revolutionary Marxists are in no way opposed to an alliance between the proletariat and the working, non-exploitative petty bourgeoisie of the towns and countryside, even in those countries where they are in a minority. In many imperialist countries, such as Portugal, Spain, Italy and France, the establishment of the workers and peasants alliance is still very important, politically and above all economically, for the victory and the consolidation of the socialist revolution.

What we dispute is that an alliance between working class parties and bourgeois parties is necessary in order to reach a similar alliance among the labouring classes. On the contrary, the liberation of the peasantry and the urban petty bourgeoisie from the hold of the bourgeoisie also presupposes their emancipation from the support they tend to give to bourgeois political parties. The alliance can and ought to be based on common interests. The proletariat and its parties should offer these classes the social, economic, cultural and political objectives which concern them, and which the bourgeoisie is incapable of achieving. If experience confirms the will of the proletariat to seize power and implement its programme, it can obtain the support of a large part of the petty bourgeoisie who wish to achieve these objectives.

7 The liberation movements of women and oppressed national minorities in the rise of anti-capitalist struggles

The organised labour movement has traditionally posed the problem of 'alliances' either in electoral and political terms (alliance between different parties) or in terms of the alliance of the working class with the working peasantry and other exploited layers of the petty bourgeoisie. But the combination of social revolution and the liberation movement of oppressed nationalities has already played an important role in the great proletarian revolutions of the past — above all in the Russian and Spanish revolutions.

As late capitalism becomes inextricably linked with an increasingly generalised social crisis (essentially since the second half of the 1960s), social-political struggles in the imperialist countries are characterised by a combination of 'pure' working class struggles and explosions of discontent and social revolt on the part of large sectors of the population whose composition is not entirely proletarian: youth in rebellion, the women's liberation movement, the revolt of oppressed nationalities.

When we say 'not entirely proletarian in composition' we mean exactly that. It is absurd to describe the youth, women, or racial and ethnic minorities as 'non-proletarian' or even 'petty-bourgeois' as a whole on the basis of ideological or psychological criteria. A growing part of the female population in the imperialist countries (in some cases more than 50 per cent) is made up of women workers and not housewives. A large number of the youth are young workers or apprentices. The Blacks, Puerto Ricans and Chicanos in the USA; the Irish, Asian and West Indian immigrants in Britain; the Basques and Catalans in Spain — to give only these three examples — are not only mainly working class themselves; they actually form a considerable part of the working class as a whole in these states.

In fact, the conditions of existence and special demands of all the layers in specific revolt — women, youth, racial and national minorities — require the special attention of the workers movement and its revolutionary vanguard for three obvious reasons.

First, these layers include in general the most exploited and poorest section of the world proletariat. That, if for no other reason, already demands the particular attention of every conscious worker. Secondly, these layers are in general victims of a double oppression, both as workers and as women, youth, minorities, immigrants, etc. And the proletariat cannot finally free itself, and, above all, cannot abolish wage labour and construct a classless society, unless it radically eliminates *all* forms of discrimination, oppression, and social inequality. Thirdly, the rebellion and fight for liberation of these layers allows us to win to the struggle for the socialist revolution those non-proletarian sectors who make up part of the oppressed layers mentioned above.

This alliance is obviously not automatic. It depends on the extent of the class divide that the extreme polarisation of social forces in the course of the revolutionary process will inevitably provoke inside the liberation movements of women, of youth, of oppressed nationalities and races. But it also depends on the ability of the workers movement, and above all its revolutionary vanguard, to take boldly in hand the just cause for which these oppressed layers are fighting.

Revolutionary Marxists recognise as justified the autonomous liberation movements of women, of youth, of oppressed nationalities and races — not only before but even after the overthrow of capitalism, which will not remove in one day the vestiges of thousands of years of sexist, racist, chauvinistic and xenophobic prejudices inside the working masses. They will strive inside these autonomous mass movements to be the best fighters for all just and progressive demands, to promote the largest and most unitary mobilisations and struggles.

At the same time, they will fight systematically for those overall political and social solutions — the taking of power by the working class; the abolition of the capitalist system — without which there can be no general and lasting solution to sexist, racist and chauvinist discrimination. They will advocate no less sytematically the solidarity of all the exploited and all the workers in the struggle for their class interests, independently of all differences of sex, race, or nationality. The more firm and determined their struggle against all the special forms of oppression suffered by these super-exploited layers, the more effective will be this struggle for general class solidarity within them.

1 The socialist goal

Our socialist objective is the replacement of bourgeois society, based on the struggle of all against all, by a classless community in which social solidarity replaces the search for individual wealth as the essential motive for action, and in which the wealth of society assures the harmonious development of all individuals.

Far from wanting 'to make everyone the same', as the ignorant opponents of socialism pretend, Marxists want to allow the development for the first time in human history of the whole infinite range of different possibilities of thought and action present in each individual. But they understand that *social and economic equality*, the emancipation of humanity from the necessity to fight for its daily bread, represents a precondition for achieving the true realisation of the human personality in all individuals.

A socialist society therefore requires an economy developed to the point where *production for need* supersedes production for *profit*. Socialist humanity will no longer produce goods to be exchanged for money on the market. It will produce use values distributed to all members of society in order to satisfy their needs.

Such a society will liberate humanity from the chains of the social and economic division of labour. Marxists reject the thesis according to which certain people 'are born to command' and others 'born to obey'. Nobody is by nature marked out to be a miner, a miller or a bus conductor for the whole of their life. The desire to engage in a certain number of different activities exists in everybody: you only have to see what workers do in their leisure time to understand this. In socialist society the high level of technical and intellectual skills of every citizen will allow them to set about numerous and varied tasks during their life, all useful to the community. The choice of a job will no longer be imposed on people by material forces or conditions independently of their own wishes. It will depend on their own needs, their own individual development.

Work will cease to be an *imposed burden* one tries to avoid, and will become simply the fulfilment of the personality. Humanity will finally be free in the real sense of the word. Such a society will try to eliminate all the sources of conflict between human beings. The immense resources wasted today in destruction and repression will be turned to the struggle against disease, to the upbringing of children, to education and to the arts. Eliminating all the social and economic antagonisms between people, this society will eliminate all the causes of war and violent conflict. Only the establishment in the entire world of a socialist society can guarantee to humanity the universal peace that is required even for its survival as a species in the epoch of atomic and thermo-nuclear weapons.

2 The economic and social conditions for the attainment of this goal

If we do not limit ourselves to dreaming of a radiant future, if we intend to fight for this future, we must understand that the construction of a socialist society (which will completely overthrow the habits and customs established for thousands of years in class-divided societies) will have to be subordinated to equally staggering material transformations which must first of all be brought about.

The achieving of socialism requires above all the suppression of the private ownership of the means of production. In the epoch of large-scale industry and modern techniques (which one cannot abandon without throwing humanity back into generalised poverty), this private ownership of the means of production inevitably involves the division of society into a minority of capitalists who exploit and a majority of wage-earners who are exploited.

The achieving of socialist society demands the suppression of the wage-earning relationship as such, of the sale of labour power for a fixed money-wage, which reduces the producer to a powerless cog in economic life. The remuneration of labour through free access to all the goods required to satisfy the needs of the producers should be progressively substituted for the earning of wages. It is only in a society which assures people such an *abundance of goods* that a new social consciousness, a new attitude between people and towards work, can be born.

Such an abundance of goods is in no way utopian so long as it is gradually introduced, starting from a progressive rationalisation of people's needs once they have been emancipated from poverty, from the constraints of competition, from the race for private enrichment, and from the advertising manipulations which seek to create a permanent state of dissatisfaction in individuals. Thus progress in the standard of living has already created a situation where all but the poorest people in the imperialist countries can eat all they want of bread, potatoes, vegetables, some fruits and even dairy products and pork meat. A similar tendency can be seen with underwear, shoes, basic furniture, etc. — at least in the richest countries. All these products could be progressively distributed free of charge, without making use of money and without adding significantly to collective spending. The same possibility exists for social services such as teaching, health care, public transport, etc.

But the abolition of wage-labour requires not merely the transformation of the conditions of remuneration and of distribution of goods. It also means doing away with *the hierarchical structure of the factory* and the substitution of a system of producers' democracy for the sole instructions of the boss (assisted by workshop managers, foremen, etc.). The aim of socialism is self-government on all levels of social life, beginning with economic life. It is the replacement of all institutional hierarchies by elected delegates, of all permanent functionaries by delegates who take on these functions in turn. It is in this way that we will be able to establish the conditions for true equality.

Social wealth which allows the creation of a system of plenty can only be achieved through a *planned economy* which avoids any waste such as the massive non-utilisation of the means of production or unemployment, as well as their utilisation for ends contrary to humanity's interests. The emancipation of labour remains dependent on the enormous development of modern techniques — productive use of atomic energy (under conditions of maximum security, together with intensive research for alternative sources of energy); electronic and remote control mechanisms which allow the complete automation of production — which liberate humanity more and more from heavy, degrading, soul-destroying and monotonous tasks. Thus history replies in advance to the crude old objection to socialism: 'Who would do the dirty jobs in a socialist society?'

The maximum development of production in the most favourable conditions for humanity will require the maintenance and extension of the international division of labour (profoundly altered, however, in order to bring an end to the 'advanced'/'dependent' relationship between countries), the abolition of frontiers, and the planning of the whole of the world economy. The abolition of frontiers and the real unification of the human race is, moreover, also a psychological requirement of socialism, the only means of suppressing economic and social inequality between nations. The abolition of frontiers in no way means the suppression of the cultural identity of each nation; on the contrary, it will permit the assertion of this identity in a more striking fashion than today, and on its own terms.

The management of factories by the workers, of the economy by a congress of workers' councils, of all spheres of social life by the relevant collectivity, also depends upon certain material conditions for its fulfilment. *The radical reduction of the working day* — in fact, the introduction of the half day at work — is absolutely necessary to give the producers time to manage the factories and the communities, and to prevent the emergence of a new layer of professional administrators.

The generalisation of higher education — and a new distribution of 'study time' and 'work time' across the whole of men and women's adult life — is vital for the gradual disappearance of the separation between manual and intellectual labour. *Strict equality of remuneration, of representation and of opportunities for obtaining new skills* is necessary to ensure that the inequality between the sexes is not maintained after the disappearance of the inequality between social classes.

3 The political, ideological, psychological and cultural conditions for the attainment of this goal

The material conditions for the arrival of a classless society are necessary but not sufficient. Socialism and communism will not be the automatic product of the development of the productive forces, the disappearance of poverty, and the raising of the level of technical and intellectual skills of humanity. It will also be necessary to alter the habits, morals, and ways of thinking which have resulted from thousands of years of exploitation, oppression and social conditions favouring the desire for private enrichment.

Above all, it will be necessary to remove all political power from the dominant classes and to prevent them from getting it back. The general arming of the workers, replacing the permanent armies, and then the progressive destruction of all arms, making it impossible for any partisans of a re-establishment of minority rule to produce these arms, should allow us to achieve this aim.

The democracy of workers' councils; the exercise of all political power by these councils; public control of production and the distribution of wealth; the widest public debate on all matters involving major political and economic decisions; access for all workers to the means of information and all organs of public opinion: all this should ensure once and for all that no return to a regime of oppression and exploitation is any longer possible.

Then it will be a matter of creating suitable conditions for the workers *to get used to* the new security of their existence and stop *measuring* their efforts in terms of a specific and expected return. This psychological revolution can only take place when experience has taught people that socialist society can guarantee effectively — and permanently — the satisfaction of all their basic needs, without having to balance this up against each person's contribution to the social wealth.

Free food and basic clothing; public services; health care; education; cultural services — these will allow us to attain this goal after two or three generations have experienced them. Thenceforth work will no longer be considered as a means of 'earning a living' but will become a necessary creative activity through which everyone contributes to the well-being and development of all.

The radical transformation of such structures of oppression as the patriarchal family, the authoritarian school, and the passive consumption of ideas and 'culture' will go hand in hand with these social and political transformations.

The dictatorship of the proletariat will suppress no idea and no scientific, philosophical, religious, literary, cultural or artistic current. It will not be afraid of ideas, having full confidence in the superiority of communist ideas. It will not, for all that, be neutral in the ideological struggle which follows; it will establish all the conditions suitable for the emancipated proletariat to assimilate the best products of the old culture and progressively build the elements of the unified communist culture of future humanity.

The cultural revolution which will set its seal on the construction of communism will mean above all a revolution in the conditions in which humanity creates its culture, the transformation of the mass of people from passive consumers into active cultural producers and creators.

The biggest obstacle which remains to be surmounted in the creation of a communist world is the enormous gap which separates the *per capita* production and standard of living of inhabitants of the advanced industrial countries from those of the under-developed countries. Marxism decisively rejects the reactionary utopia of an ascetic communism of poverty. The flowering of the economic and social life of the peoples of these regions requires not only the socialist planning of the world economy but also a radical redistribution of material resources in favour of these peoples.

Only a transformation of the egotistical, short-sighted and petty-bourgeois ways of thinking which survive today among important sections of the working class in the West will enable us to achieve this goal. Internationalist education will have to go hand in hand with the adjustment to abundance, which will show that such a redistribution can take place without leading to a reduction in the living standards of the Western masses.

4 The stages of the classless society

On the basis of the already rich experience of more than a century of proletarian revolution — that is, since the Paris Commune — three stages can be distinguished in the construction of a classless society:

— *The stage of transition from capitalism to socialism*, the stage of the dictatorship of the proletariat, of the survival of capitalism in important countries, of the partial survival of commodity production and the money economy, of the survival of different classes and social layers within the countries involved in this stage, and therefore of the necessary survival of the state to defend the interests of the workers against the partisans of a return to the rule of capital.

— *The stage of socialism*, whose construction completes and is characterised by the disappearance of social classes ('socialism is the classless society', said Lenin), by the withering away of the commodity and money economy, by the withering away of the state, by the international triumph of the new society. However, in the socialist stage the remuneration of everyone (apart, of course, from the free satisfaction of basic needs) will continue to be measured in terms of the quantity of labour given to society.

— *The stage of communism*, characterised by the complete application of the principle 'from each according to their ability, to each according to their needs', by the disappearance of the social division of labour, by the disappearance of the separation of town and country. Humanity will reorganise itself into free communes of producer-consumers, capable of administering themselves without any separate organ for this purpose, at one with a restored natural habitat and protected from any threat of destruction of the ecological balance.

However, in a post-capitalist society where the workers and not a bureaucratic layer hold effective power, there will be no need of revolutions and similar sudden shifts to move from one stage to the next. They will result from the progressive evolution of production and social relations. They will be the expression of the progressive withering away of commodity categories, of money, of social classes, of the state, of the social division of labour, and of the thought processes which resulted from the inequality and social struggles of the past. The main thing is immediately *to begin* these processes of withering away and not to leave them to future generations.

Such is our communist ideal. It constitutes the only solution to the burning problems with which humanity is confronted. To devote one's life to its realisation, and therefore to build the Fourth International, is to live up to the intelligence and generosity of the best sons and daughters of our species, the most daring thinkers of the past, the most courageous fighters for the emancipation of labour — from Spartacus leading the Roman slaves' revolt to those who led the peasant wars against serfdom, from the heroes of the Paris Commune to those of the Red Army, from the *milicianos* who in July 1936 beat the fascists in Barcelona, Madrid and nearly all the big industrial cities of Spain to the heroic Vietnamese who in a thirty years' war defeated Japanese, French and American imperialism.

Chapter 16
Materialist Dialectics

1 Universal motion

If we go back over the fifteen preceding chapters and try to sum up their content in one formula, we can arrive only at this: everything changes and is in perpetual motion.

Humanity moves from primitive classless society to a society divided into classes; this in turn gives way to the classless socialist society of tomorrow. Modes of production succeed one another; even before disappearing, they are subject to constant changes. Today's ruling class is very different from the class of slave-owners who dominated the Roman Empire. The contemporary proletariat is totally different from the medieval serfs. There is a whole world of difference between the small manufacturing capitalist of the early Nineteenth Century and Mr Rockefeller or the boss of the Rhône-Poulenc trust today. Everything changes, everything is in perpetual motion.

We find this universal motion at all levels of reality, not just that of the history of human societies. Individuals change, subject to an inexorable destiny. They are born, grow, mature, become adult, then they start to decline and finally they die. This destiny affects living species as it affects individuals. The human species has not always existed. Species which populated our planet a long time ago, like the giant reptiles of the tertiary period, have disappeared. Other vegetable and animal species are disappearing at this moment under our very eyes, partly as a result of the anarchic and barbarous disturbances that the capitalist mode of production has brought about in the ecology of the Earth.

Our planet itself will not survive for ever. The law of energy loss condemns it to inevitable disappearance some day. It has not always existed. It will not always exist. It is the product of an inter-planetary constellation which is itself only one of countless similar constellations in the universe.

Motion, universal evolution, governs all existence. This is material. The basic component of matter is the atom, which is itself composed of even smaller particles. Atoms in combination form molecules, which together form the basic elements of the Earth's surface and atmosphere. For instance, oxygen and hydrogen combined together in a determined form, H_2O, constitute water; other molecules form the metals, acids and bases.

In a determined set of conditions, the evolution of inorganic matter brought about the birth of organic matter. This produced the evolution of the vegetable and animal living species. In the course of this evolution higher living species, the mammals, have evolved. One of the mammal species, the simians, has gone through an evolution culminating in the birth of a new species, the human species.

2 Dialectics, the logic of motion

Since universal motion governs all existence it would seem possible to find common characteristics in the motion of matter, that of human society, and that of human knowledge. In fact, the materialist dialectics of Marx and Engels claims to reveal these common characteristics.

The dialectics or the logic of motion is manifested on three levels:

• The dialectics of nature, which are entirely objective — that is, independent of human plans, intentions and motivations. This does not negate the fact that with the development of the productive forces, humanity can use the laws of nature to improve its conditions of survival, reproduction and self-fulfilment.

• The dialectics of history, which were at first largely objective, but in which the eruption of the revolutionary project of the proletariat to reconstruct society according to a predetermined plan constitutes a revolutionary change — although the elaboration and realisation of this project is linked to objective and already existing material and social conditions, independent of human will.

• The dialectics of knowledge (of human thought), which

are object/subject dialectics, the result of the constant interaction between the objects to be understood (objects of all the sciences) and the action of the subjects who try to understand them (and who are conditioned by their social situation, the means of investigation at their disposal — their instruments of labour as much as their thought concepts — the transformation of these means by current social activity, etc.).

Inasmuch as the *discovery* of the objective dialectic is itself a phase in the history of human thought and knowledge (the dialectic was first elaborated by Greek philosophers such as Heraclites, then taken up by Spinoza and perfected by Hegel and Marx), one could be tempted to reduce all dialectics to the object/subject relation. This would be an error. It is true that everything we know, including our knowledge of the dialectics of nature, we have learnt through the intermediary of our brain and our social praxis. It is also true that our ideas and our social praxis are determined by our social conditions of existence. But this obvious fact does not prevent us from knowing — verifying and seeing confirmed by many practical proofs — that life is older than human thought, that the Earth is older than life, that the universe is older than the Earth, that this motion is independent of human action, thought or existence. This is the precise sense of the notion of objective materialist dialectics.

As our knowledge is extended and becomes more scientific; as it comes closer to reality (*total* identity of knowledge with reality is impossible, mainly because the latter is in perpetual motion), its progress follows more closely the objective motion of matter. The dialectics of our scientific thought, materialist dialectics, can grasp reality precisely because its own motion increasingly corresponds to the motion of matter. In other words, the laws of knowledge and the method of understanding reality employed by materialist dialectics increasingly correspond to the actual laws governing the universal motion of objective reality.

It is necessary to point out an important difference between the development of the natural sciences and that of the social sciences, by which we mean knowledge concerning social life as the object of research, taking in our understanding of the origins and the dialectics of development of all the sciences, including the natural sciences. For the development of the natural sciences is also historically and socially determined. Even the most intrepid geniuses can only pose and resolve a certain number of scientific problems in any one epoch. They are the offshoots of received ideas and education. New problematics appear in this context, in relation to material transformation, especially with regard to labour, instruments of labour, tools of scientific investigation, etc. This is, however, a question of *indirect* determination, not immediately mediated by material class interests.

It is rather different with the social sciences. These are much more deeply related to the organisation and structure of class society. Here the weight of 'received ideas and education' is much greater, in that these ideas are simply *the expression*, on the ideological level, of the *interests* of either social conservation or social revolution, interests which can be reduced to antagonistic class positions. Without wishing to transform philosophers, historians, economists, sociologists and anthropologists into deliberate 'agents' of this or that social class, engaged in a 'conspiracy' either to defend the established order or to 'organise subversion', it is evident that the social determination of the development of the social sciences is much more direct and immediate than that of the natural sciences. In the same way, and because of the way things are, the *object* of the social sciences is much more *immediately* determined by the structure and history of the societies to which the facts studied refer, which is not the case with the object of the natural sciences.

3 Dialectics and formal logic

Dialectics, or the logic of motion, is distinct from formal or static logic. Formal logic is based on three fundamental laws:

(a) The law of identity: A is equal to A; a thing is always equal to itself.

(b) The law of contradiction: A is different from non-A; A can never equal non-A.

(c) The law of exclusion: either A, or non-A; nothing can be neither A nor non-A.

A moment's reflection will allow us to conclude that formal

logic is characterised by the thought process which consists of putting motion, change, into parentheses. All the laws enumerated above are true, *so long as we abstract from motion*. A will remain A so long as it does not change. A is different from non-A so long as it is not transformed into its opposite. A and non-A exclude each other so long as there is no movement which *combines* A and non-A, etc. These laws are obviously insufficient if we consider the *transformation* of the chrysalid into the butterfly, the passage of the adolescent into the adult, the *movement* of life into death, the *birth* of a new species or a new social order, the *combination* of two cells into a new one, etc.

From two points of view it is useful to abstract from motion, transformation and change: firstly, to be able to study phenomena continually in an isolated state, which allows us to improve our knowledge of these phenomena; secondly, from a practical point of view, when the changes taking place are of an infinitesimal nature, and can therefore be neglected by ordinary practice concerned with them.

If I buy a kilo of prepacked sugar at the grocers, the equation of balance 'one kilo of sugar = one kilo' is of value to me, given the practical purpose of my purchase. When sugaring my coffee or balancing my housekeeping money, the fact that the real weight of such a packet may not actually be 1 kilo but 999.8 grammes, and the weight of another packet 990 grammes, is of no importance. From a practical point of view, such small differences can well be neglected.

That is why formal logic continues to be used in both theory and practice. That is why materialist dialectics does not challenge formal logic but absorbs it, seeing it as a valuable instrument of analysis and knowledge. It is valuable as long as we are clear about its limits, as long as we understand that it cannot be applied to phenomena of motion, to processes of change. As soon as we are dealing with such phenomena, the use of dialectical categories, those of the logic of motion, different from the categories of formal logic, is imposed on us.

4 Motion, a function of contradiction

By its nature, movement is passage and overtaking. From a

static point of view, an object cannot be in two different places at the same moment (even if it is an infinitely short moment). From a dynamic point of view, the motion of an object is precisely its passage from one point to another.

The dialectics or logic of motion therefore study primarily the laws of motion and the forms adopted by it. These are examined from two aspects: motion as a function of contradiction; motion as a function of totality.

All motion has a cause. Causality is one of the fundamental categories of dialectics, as it is of all sciences. In the final analysis, to deny causality is to deny the possibility of knowledge.

A fundamental cause of all motion, all change, is the internal contradictions of the changing object. In the final analysis, every object, every phenomenon, changes, moves, is transformed and modified under the influence of its internal contradictions. In this sense, dialectics has often been correctly called the science of contradictions. The logic of motion and the logic of contradiction are two practically identical definitions of dialectics.

The study of every object, phenomenon or set of phenomena ought to have as its aim the discovery of its constituent contradictory elements, and of the motion and dynamic unleashed by these contradictions.

Thus, throughout this little book, we have indicated at what point class struggle, resulting from the existence of antagonistic social classes within society, governs movement, change, in societies divided into classes. On a larger scale, encompassing primitive classless society, society divided into classes, and the future socialist society, we can say that the contradiction between the level attained at certain epochs by the development of the productive forces (the degree of human control over nature) and the relations of production (social organisation), which in the last analysis arises from the previous levels of development of these same productive forces — that this contradiction governs the evolution of humanity.

By simplifying, we can discern the following basic laws of motion, the principal forms they take and which constitute the fundamental categories of dialectical logic, the logic of motion:

(a) *The unity and contradiction of opposites*. Motion is contradiction. Contradiction is the co-existence of elements opposed to each other, simultaneous co-existence and opposition between these elements. If there is integral homogeneity, a total absence of elements opposed to each other, there is no contradiction, no motion, no life, no existence.

The existence of contradictory elements includes both their co-existence in a structured totality, in a whole in which each element has its place, and the struggle by these elements to break up this whole. Capitalism is not possible without the *simultaneous* existence of capital and wage labour, of the bourgeoisie and the proletariat. The one cannot exist without the other. But this in no way means that the one is not constantly trying to throw off the other, that the proletariat is not trying to suppress capital and wage-earning, trying therefore to supplant capitalism, that capitalism has not the tendency to supplant living labour (wage labour) by 'dead labour' (machinery).

(b) *Quantitative and qualitative change*. Motion can take the form of changes which maintain the structure (or the quality) of the given phenomenon. In this case we talk about a quantitative change, which is often imperceptible. The structure remains in equilibrium. At a certain threshold, quantitative change is transformed into qualitative change. Beyond this threshold, change ceases to be gradual, and appears in the form of 'leaps'. Equilibrium gives way to disequilibrium, evolution to revolution, till a new equilibrium is reached. A new 'quality' appears. A small village can gradually change into a big village, and even into a small town. But there is not merely a quantitative difference between a large town and a village (number of inhabitants, amount of built up area), as a result of the 'urban revolution'. There is also a qualitative difference. The professional activity of the majority of the inhabitants has been altered. The largest group no longer consists of agriculturalists, but of artisans, merchants, functionaries. A new social milieu is formed, posing social problems which had hitherto not existed in the village: problems of transportation, communication, social services, 'specialised' areas, etc. New social classes appear, with new contradictions between them.

(c) *Negation and surpassing.* All motion tends to produce the negation of certain phenomena, tends to transform objects into their opposite. Life produces death. Heat can only be understood in relation to cold. 'Every determination is a negation', stated that great dialectician Spinoza. Classless society produces class society, which in turn produces a new classless society on a higher level. But we must distinguish between 'pure' negation and 'negation of the negation', that is, the transcending of the contradiction, which implies at the same time negation, conservation and elevation to a higher level. Primitive classless society had a high level of internal cohesion, which was precisely a function of its poverty, its almost total subordination to the forces of nature. Society divided into classes is a stage in the growing domination of the forces of nature by humanity, paid for at the cost of a profound contradiction and tearing apart of the social organisation. In the future socialist society this negation will be transcended. This time, even higher mastery of humanity over the forces of nature will be combined with an equally superior form of social cohesion and co-operation, thanks to the existence of a classless society.

5 *Some further problems of the dialectics of knowledge*

(a) *Content and form.* All motion necessarily takes successive forms (structures) which can vary according to a large number of circumstances. It cannot automatically throw off any form previously adopted. The form resists. This resistance must be broken. The form should correspond to the content, and up to a certain point it does. But its more petrified nature opposes any absolute and permanent correspondence with movement, which is itself the opposite of anything which is fixed and constant.

A good example of this contradictory relationship between form and content is furnished by the *dialectic between the relations of production and the productive forces.* In order to develop, the productive forces must necessarily be inserted in certain forms of human social organisation: slave, feudal, capitalist relations of production, etc. At first, each new form of the organisation of labour and production (superior to the preceding form from the point of view of the average productivity of labour) stimulates the growth of the productive forces. But at a certain stage it becomes itself a hindrance to further growth. It must, therefore, be broken down and replaced by a new set of relations of production which are superior again, in order to pave the way for a new 'great leap forward' in the material and intellectual progress of humanity.

(b) *Cause and effect*. All movement appears to be a tangled chain of causes and effects. At first glance, an inextricable interaction mixes them up together. The wage-earning proletariat develops because of the private appropriation of the means of production, which have become the monopoly of one social class. But this monopoly is maintained as the result of the existence of the wage-earners.

Their wages do not permit the workers to acquire the means of production. The wage-earners produce surplus value which is appropriated by the capitalists and is transformed into the bourgeois ownership of even more means of production. And so it goes on, turning cause into effect and effect into cause. In order to emerge from this *imbroglio* and to avoid falling into pointless eclecticism, we must apply the genetic method, that is, look for the *historical origin* of the movement in question. Thus one finds that capital and surplus value do in fact pre-date the wage-earning proletariat, and were developed outside the sphere of production; that there was a *primitive accumulation* of capital which breaks up the apparent vicious circle: wage-earners — capital — wage-earners.

(c) *Means and goals*. All conscious movement or activity is directed towards the realisation of a certain goal. Thought processes are instruments for attempting to eliminate obstacles on the road towards such goals. *Efficient* thought processes (from the simplest 'individual' solution of daily practical questions to the highest forms of 'pure science') are in the last analysis measured by the degree to which they enable one to approach or to realise the given goal.

But there is an obvious dialectical interaction between means and goals. All individual and social actions have innumerable effects. While some of them have been foreseen, others have not. Some of the unforeseen effects might very well make the realisation of the given goal more difficult instead of facilitating it. Only *certain* means, the *sum total* of whose effects will actually bring us nearer to the goal, are efficient from that point of view. And the very goal might become transformed by sticking to means which push the realisation of the initial goal further and further into the future (the historical tragedies of reformism and Stalinism in the organised labour movement are excellent illustrations of this law).

Furthermore, means and goals of *social* action are not arbitrarily arrived at by humanity, and of 'pure free will'. They emerge under given social and material constraints, in function of given social interests. Goals are fixed in function of *needs* which are not independent from the social framework and the material infrastructure. Means are chosen in function of experience and invention (imagination), which likewise are not unrelated to social conditions and activities. *Both* the capacity for fixing goals (including inventing new ones), and the constraints which imprison the choices of goals and means, characterise the dialectics of knowledge (see Chapter 17, Section 5, for an application of this general rule to the problem of socialism).

(d) *The general and the specific*. Each movement, each phenomenon, has characteristics which are specific to it. At the same time, and in spite of these particularities, no movement or phenomenon can be grasped, understood and explained except within the framework of larger and more general entities. British Nineteenth Century capitalism is not identical to British capitalism in the second half of the Twentieth Century, nor the American capitalism of today. Each one of these represents a specific social formation with a specific insertion in a world economy which has greatly changed in the course of a century. Nevertheless, neither British capitalism of the Victorian epoch, nor the decadent British capitalism of today, nor contemporary American capitalism, can be understood outside of the general laws of development which characterise capitalism as a system. The dialectic of the general and the specific is not just a matter of 'combining' the analysis of the 'general' with that of the 'specific'. It also tries to explain the specific in relation to the general laws, and modifies the general laws through the intervention of a certain number of specific factors.

(e) *The relative and the absolute*. To understand motion, universal change, is also to understand the existence of an infinite number of transitory situations. ('Movement is the unity of continuity and discontinuity.') That is why one of the fundamental characteristics of dialectics is the understanding of the relativity of things, the refusal to erect *absolute* barriers between categories, the attempt to find *mediating forces* between opposing elements. Universal evolution implies the existence of hybrid phenomena, of situations and cases of 'transition' between life and death, between vegetable and animal species, between birds and mammals, between apes and humans, which render the distinctions between all these categories relative.

However, dialectics has often been used in a subjectivist manner, as the 'art of confusion' or the 'art of defending paradoxes'. The difference between scientific dialectics, an instrument for the understanding of objective reality, and *sophistry* or subjective dialectics, is mainly that the relativity of phenomena and categories in itself becomes something absolute with the sophists. They forget, or pretend to forget, that the relativity of categories is only partial relativity and not absolute relativity, and that, in turn, *it is equally necessary to make relativity relative*.

According to scientific dialectics, the 'absolute' difference between life and death is negated by the existence of transitory situations. Everything is relative and hence also the difference between life and death, reply the sophists. No, answers the dialectician: there is also something absolute and not just something relative in the difference between life and death. We should not come to the absurd conclusion which denies that death is the negation of life, by using the undeniable fact that there are many intermediary stages.

6 Motion as a function of totality — the abstract and the concrete

We have seen that all motion is a function of the internal contradictions of the phenomenon or set of phenomena under consideration. Each phenomenon — whether it be a living cell, a natural milieu where various species exist, a human society, an interplanetary system, or an atom — contains an infinite number of aspects, ingredients and constituent elements. These elements are not assembled by chance in a constantly changing manner. They constitute *structured wholes*, a *totality*, an organic system constructed according to an intrinsic logic.

For instance, within bourgeois society, the mutual and antagonistic relations between capital and labour have nothing to do with chance. They are determined by the economic obligation of the wage-earners to sell their labour power to the capitalists, the owners of the means of production and subsistence, which have both taken the form of commodities. Mutual relations qualitatively different from these structures characterize other societies based on exploitation, which are therefore not capitalist societies.

Materialist dialectics must absorb each phenomenon, each object of analysis and comprehension, not just in order to determine the internal contradictions which determine its evolution (its laws of motion). It must also attempt to approach this phenomenon globally, to grasp it in *all* its aspects, to consider it in its totality, to avoid any unilateral approach which isolates in an arbitrary manner a particular aspect of reality and no less arbitrarily suppresses another, and is hence incapable of grasping the contradictions in their entirety, and therefore also of understanding *the movement in its totality*.

This ability of dialectics to integrate the universalist approach into its analysis is one of its principal merits. 'Logic of motion', 'logic of contradiction' and 'logic of totality' are practically synonymous definitions of dialectics. It is when they close their eyes to certain contradictory elements of reality which they think would make analysis 'too complex' that undialectical thinkers pass from the total to the partial, throwing out both contradiction and totality at the same time.

Of course, a certain amount of simplification, a certain 'reduction' of the 'totality' to its *decisive* constituent elements, is inevitable as the *first step* in approaching any phenomenon for scientific analysis, which is at first always necessarily abstract. But we have to remember that this inevitable process of abstraction also impoverishes reality. The nearer one approaches to reality, the nearer one comes to a totality rich in an infinite number of aspects that scientific analysis, knowledge, should explain in both their reciprocal relations and their contradictory relations. 'Truth is always concrete' (Lenin). 'Truth is the totality' (Hegel).

7 Theory and practice

Dialectics is a method, an instrument of knowledge. Historically, one can define materialist dialectics as the proletariat's theory of knowledge (this in no way questions its objectively scientific character, which also requires constant verification on the scientific terrain as well). Every theory of knowledge is put to an implacable test: that of practical experience.

In the last analysis, knowledge itself is not a phenomenon which is detached from the life and interests of humanity. It is a weapon in the conservation of the species, an instrument which enables humanity the better to dominate the forces of nature, to understand the origins of the 'social question' and the ways to solve it. *Knowledge is, therefore, born of the social practice of humanity; its function is to perfect this practice.* In the last analysis, its effectiveness is measured by its practical results. Practical verification remains the best final weapon against the sophists and the sceptics.

That is not to say that the theory disappears into vulgar short-sighted pragmatism. Very often the practical effectiveness, the 'true' or 'false' character of a scientific hypothesis, does not immediately appear. It needs time, feedback, new experiences, a successive series of 'practical tests', before it proves itself effectively in practice. In spite of the best intentions and convictions, many men and women, impressionistic prisoners of appearances, of a partial and superficial view of reality, of a temporary view of the historical process (which is itself finally determined by the ideology of non-revolutionary classes and social layers), may doubt the bourgeois character of parliamentary democracy, doubt the need for the dictatorship of the proletariat, or the need for a victorious international revolution to complete the construction of a truly socialist society in the USSR and any other country.

But, in the end, facts will confirm which theory was really scientific, capable of grasping reality in all its contradictions, in its movement as a totality, and which hypotheses were wrong, capable of grasping only parts of the reality, isolating them from the structured totality, and therefore incapable of grasping the movement in the long term in its fundamental logic.

The victory of the world socialist revolution, the arrival of a classless society, will confirm in practice the validity of revolutionary Marxist theory.

We can now formulate in a more systematic manner the fundamental tenets of historical materialism, which have already been touched on briefly in the first chapters of this little book.

1 Human production and human communications

This creature which has become man is a unique animal both because of its physical qualities and because of its physical deficiencies. On the one hand there is the upright stance, the hand with a free and flexible thumb, the protruding eyes which afford stereoscopic vision, the tongue, throat and vocal chords which permit the articulation of separate and combined sounds, the highly developed cortex, frontal lobe of the brain and cerebral convolutions, the cranial casing, and the reduced facial surface which allows these developments. All these physical qualities are indispensable for the deliberate fabrication of tools, and have been progressively perfected as tools and productive work have been perfected.

 On the other hand, most of the human senses and organs are less developed than those of other highly specialised animal species. When forced, possibly because of a change in climate, to come down from the trees and live off a varied diet in the savanna, primitive humanity could not defend itself from the carnivores by running like an antelope, by climbing like a chimpanzee, by flying away like a bird, or by depending on its physical strength like a buffalo or a gorilla. With such physical characteristics it could not lay its hands on the most alluring foodstuffs: the countless ruminants with whom it shared the savanna. Above all, the new-born human was particularly vulnerable and helpless, really an extra-uterine embryo totally dependent on the mothers in the horde (the upright stance, which narrowed the pelvis in the female, undoubtedly contributed to this premature characteristic in human childbirth).

Both the *possibility* of and the *need* for *social organisation* are rooted in this combination of qualities and deficiencies. Humans cannot survive individually or ensure their subsistence without co-operation with other members of their species. Their physical organs are too little developed to allow them to appropriate their foodstuffs directly. Humans must *produce* these collectively, with the aid of tools, prolonging and perfecting their organs. This production is ensured through communal action by groups of humans. Human infants are integrated into the group and learn the rules and techniques of survival as members of the group through their progressive socialisation.

The social organisation of humans and the socialisation of human infants presupposes qualitatively superior forms of communication between the members of the group to those existing among other animal species. These superior forms of language, linked to the development of the cortex, make possible the growth of the capacities of abstraction and of learning — that is, the conservation transmission and accumulation of the lessons of experience. They make possible the production of concepts, of thought, of consciousness. In this sense, the different characteristics of humanity — our 'anthropological quality' — are closely linked to one another. It is because they are 'naked apes which walk in the upright position', because they remain extra-uterine embryos after their birth, that they must become deliberate tool makers, social animals developing language, storing up successive impressions and images, capable of using and perfecting them for practical ends, capable of learning, anticipating, thinking, abstracting, using imagination and invention.

The interaction, the combination of these characteristics, is decisive. There are human-like primates that use tools and occasionally even surpass their usually rudimentary level. There are several species that know instinctive forms of collective co-operation. There are just as many species exhibiting rudimentary forms of communication. But the human species is the only one which progressively makes tools in a more deliberate manner, perfecting them after they have been conceived of as such in a conscious way, on the basis of successive experiences, which are also transmitted as a result of more and more numerous and perfected communications. The development of tools liberates the mouth. The mouth perfects the language and the capacity for abstraction, which in turn allows the tools to be improved and new tools to be invented. The hand develops the brain, which, by improving the utilisation of the hand, creates the conditions for its own improvement.

Although the transformation of the anthropoid primates into humans is conditioned by the existence of an anatomical and neurological infrastructure, it cannot be reduced to this infrastructure. The 'production/communications' dialectic creates the possibility of an unlimited *development* in producing, inventing and perfecting tools and therefore in human production, of an unlimited *development* in human experience, learning and anticipation, and therefore of a practically unlimited *plasticity* and adaptability of the human species. *The material society and culture of humanity becomes its second nature.*

It follows that it is absurd to declare that any social institution (the absence of social inequality or of the state, the absence of private property) is 'contrary to human nature'. Humanity has lived and can live in the most diverse conditions. None of these institutions has proved immutable or an absolute precondition for human survival. Any affirmation that 'the aggressive instinct' dominates human evolution confuses the existence of a *tendency* (which co-exists, moreover, with its own negation — the instinct of sociability and co-operation) with its *realisation*. Prehistory and history show that there are social institutions and conditions which allow us to contain and hold back this tendency, while, in contrast, there are others which encourage its manifestation in outrageous forms.

The 'production/communications' dialectic dominates the entire human condition. Everything people do 'goes through their heads'. Human production is distinct from animal appropriation of food mainly in that it is not a purely instinctive activity. It generally constitutes the realisation of a 'plan' which first arises in the human head. Of course, this 'plan' does not just fall from the sky. It is the reproduction or recombination by the human brain of those elements and problems of that activity which are indispensable to human survival, which have been experienced and absorbed by the brain thousands of times in lived experience. But on the other hand, the ability to *recombine* concepts born in the last analysis from *social praxis* permits humanity to invent, to anticipate, to imagine changes in nature and society which have not yet occurred, which are only hypothetical and which will be realised at least partly because of this anticipation. Historical materialism is the science of human societies which basically tries to take account of and explain this production/communications dialectic.

2 Social base and superstructure

Every human society must produce in order to survive. Subsistence production — in the narrow or wide sense of the term, that is, the satisfaction of merely nutritional or of all socially recognised needs — and the manufacture of the instruments and work material necessary for this production constitutes the initial condition for any more complex social organisation or activity.

Historical materialism states that the way in which humanity organises its material production constitutes the base of all social organisation. This base in turn determines all other social activities — the administration of relations between groups of humans (mainly the appearance and development of the state), spiritual production, morals, law, religion, etc. These so-called social superstructure activities always remain attached, in one way or another, to the base.

This idea has shocked, and still shocks, many people. Homer's poetry, the Gospels, the Koran, the principles of Roman law, Shakespeare's plays, Michelangelo's painting, the Declaration of the Rights of Man, the *Communist Manifesto* itself — can all these products of spiritual endeavour really have depended on the way in which contemporary people tilled their fields and wove their cloth? To understand the tenets of historical materialism we must start off by explaining precisely what we mean by this formula.

Historical materialism in no way affirms that material production ('the economic factor') directly and immediately determines the content and form of all so-called super-structural activities. Moreover, the social base is not simply productive activity as such, and even less is it 'material production' taken in isolation. It is the social *relations* that people form in the production of their material life. In fact, historical materialism is not, therefore, economic determinism but *socio-economic* determinism.

Activities on the superstructural level do not immediately flow from these social relations of production. They are only determined by them in *the last instance*. A series of *mediations* therefore intervene between the two levels of social activity. These we will examine briefly in section three of this chapter.

Finally, if in the last analysis the social base determines phenomena and activities at the level of the superstructure, these latter can also react on the former. One illustration will show this. The state always has a precise class nature and corresponds to a definite socio-economic base. But it can partially modify this base. While saving the feudal nobility from certain economic ruin for a few centuries by tapping the revenue of other social classes, the state of the absolute monarchy (from the Sixteenth to Eighteenth Centuries in Europe) powerfully aided the substitution of the capitalist mode of production for the feudal mode of production, by developing mercantilism, colonialism, encouraging manu-facturing and the national monetary system, etc.

There are several reasons why activities on the super-structural level are in the final analysis determined by the social base. Those who control material production and the social surplus product also assure the livelihood of those who live off the social surplus product. Whether ideologues, artists and academics accept or rebel against this dependence, it still fixes the framework of their activity. The social relations of production therefore entail consequences as regards the forms of activity in the superstructural sphere, which also constitutes conditioning. The relations of production are accompanied by forms of communication which are predominant in each type of society, bringing about the appearance of predominant mental structures which condition forms of thought and artistic creation.

3 Material production and thought production

The social base/social superstructure dialectic affects the relations between material production and thought production. A more detailed study of these relations will better allow us to understand the complexity of this dialectic, and also allow us to underline the importance of its *active* element, an element which will be discussed at the end of this chapter.

Historical materialism argues that the relations of production constitute the base of all societies, onto which the social superstructure is built. In fact, these two levels concern *two distinct forms of social activity*. Material production is the fundamental object of activities at the level of the social base. Ideological (philosophical, religious, judicial, political, etc.), artistic and scientific production is the fundamental object of activity at the level of the social superstructure. Of course, the latter also encompasses the activities of the state apparatus, which are far from being confined to just the ideological domain (the problem of the state was taken up in Chapter 3). But, with this exception, the distinction we have made seems pertinent.

Historical materialism proffers *an explanation* of the evolution of each of these two spheres, of their interdependence and their reciprocal relations. This explanation combines four levels:

(a) All thought production is linked in one way or another to processes of material labour. It always operates with its own immediate material infrastructure. Some arts are initially the direct result of material labour (the magical function of primitive painting; the origins of dance in the formalisation of gestures of production; the integration of songs into production; etc.). Technological revolutions profoundly influence art, science, ideological production. Sciences such as geometry, astronomy, hydrography, biology and chemistry came about in intimate correlation with irrigation in agriculture, developed animal breeding, and emergent metallurgy. After the discovery of the technique of printing in the 15th Century and radio and television in the Twentieth Century, these techniques profoundly reconditioned not only the diffusion but even the form of ideas, as well as some of their content. The influence of electronic computers on the development of science in the last thirty years is evident.

(b) All thought production evolves according to an internal dialectic which is proper to its own history. Every philosopher, lawyer, priest or scientist starts off as a student. Through their studies, they assimilate to varying degrees concepts (or systems of concepts) which were produced by previous generations and transmitted as such to the present generation. Thought producers conserve, modify, adapt or shake up these concepts or hypotheses of work, according to production procedures that they borrow or invent within the framework of the dialectic proper to their activity. Each new generation tries to conserve, deepen or reject the answers to the questions flowing from the subject concerning them. Sometimes they invent new questions (which then demand 'revolutionary' answers: scientific, artistic, philosophical revolutions, etc.), or rediscover questions which were discarded by previous generations.

(c) But these modifications in the treatment of concepts, artistic forms, scientific hypotheses, do not come about in an arbitrary manner, no matter what the socio-historical conditions. They are instigated, conditioned, or, at the very least, furthered by the socio-economic context and needs. The evolution from animism to monotheism did not take place in small primitive communities restricted to hunting and gathering food. The scientific theory of labour-value could not be perfected before the appearance of modern capitalism. The development of mechanical physics is closely linked with the development of machines, which in turn correspond to specific social needs, etc.

These great transformations in thought production are also linked to *specific mental structures* which are predetermined by the social structures. It was not by chance that all the great attempts at social and political revolution of the Thirteenth to Seventeenth Centuries were expressed in the ideological form of religious struggles, given the primacy that religion had attained in the superstructure of feudal society. In the same way, from the second half of the Sixteenth Century onwards, the rise of the modern bourgeoisie created a mental structure which transposed individual autonomy, formal equality, and the competition of private owners of commodities into all domains of thought production (theory of natural right, pedagogic humanist concepts, German idealist philosophy, portraits and still lifes in painting, political liberalism, classical political economy, etc.).

(d) Finally, the evolution of spiritual production is determined in the last analysis by the conflict of social interests. It is a well-known fact that the works of the Encyclopaedists, Voltaire's polemics, the political philosophy of Jean-Jacques Rousseau and the works of the Eighteenth Century materialists were just so many weapons for the ascendant manufacturing bourgeoisie to use against decadent absolute monarchy and the decrepit remains of feudal society. The function played by the so-called utopian socialists, and by Marx and Engels, in developing the proletariat's consciousness of its class nature, of its position and its tasks in relation to bourgeois society, and of its interest in overthrowing it, is just as evident. Even today, one cannot doubt the function of astrology, of certain religions and mystical sects, of philosophies exalting the irrational, of racialist doctrines, or those of 'blood and land' (*Blut und Boden*) and contempt for humanity, as anti-working class and counter-revolutionary ferments favouring the birth of a pre-fascist climate.

These statements do not imply either the idea of an 'organised conspiracy' between distinct social classes and thought producers as individuals, or the idea of deliberate complicity on the part of all these producers with clearly laid out political projects. They reflect an *objective correlation* which *can* be, and sometimes is, subjectively assumed, though this is not necessarily the case. Thought producers can become the instruments of social forces without knowing it or wanting it. This just confirms that *it is social existence which determines consciousness*, and that given class interests assign a definite function to certain ideologies in the structure and evolution of any given society.

4 Productive forces, social relations of production and modes of production

Every human-made product is the result of a combination of three elements: the *object* of labour, which directly or indirectly is a raw material produced by nature; the *instrument* of labour, which is a means of production created by humanity whatever its degree of development (from the first wooden sticks and fashioned stone implements to today's most sophisticated automatic machines); the *subject* of labour — that is, the producer. Because in the last analysis labour is always social, the subject of the labour is inevitably inserted into a *social relation of production*.

Even if the object of labour and the instrument of labour are elements indispensable to all production, the social relations of production cannot be conceived of in a 'reified' manner — that is, they should not be seen as concerning relations between things, or between people and things. Social relations of production concern *relations between people*, and only relations between people. They bring together the *entirety* of the relations people establish amongst themselves in the production of their material life. The 'entirety of relations' not only signifies relations 'at the point of production', but also relations concerning the circulation and division of the various elements of the social product which are indispensable to material production (in particular, the way in which the objects of labour and the instruments of labour come to the immediate producers, the way in which they obtain their subsistence, etc.).

In general, given relations of production correspond to a given degree of development of the productive forces, to a given sophistication (amount) of the means of production, to a given technique and organisation of labour. In the age of the simplest stone tools, it was difficult to transcend the primitive communism of the horde or the tribe. Agriculture on the basis of irrigation and with the aid of iron tools created a considerable permanent surplus product which allowed the birth of a class society (slave society, society based on the

Asiatic mode of production, etc.). Agriculture based on triennial crop rotation created the material foundations for feudal society. The birth of the steam engine definitively assured the upsurge of modern industrial capitalism. It is difficult to imagine generalised automation without the withering away of commodity production and the money economy, that is to say, outside of a fully developed and stablised socialist society.

But if there is a *general* correspondence between the degree of development of the productive forces and the social relations of production, this correspondence is *neither absolute nor permanent*. A double incongruity between them can be produced. Given relations of production can become a great hindrance to the further growth of the productive forces: that is the clearest sign that a given social form is condemned to disappear. On the other hand, new relations of production which have just emerged from a victorious social revolution can be in advance of the degree of development of the productive forces already reached in that country. This was the case with the victorious bourgeois revolution in the Netherlands in the Sixteenth Century, and the victorious socialist revolution in Russia in October 1917.

It is not by chance that these two principal cases of incongruity concern historical periods of profound social upheaval: periods of social revolutions. Moreover, the incongruity can also lead to a long-term decline of the productive forces, as in the epoch of the decline of the Roman Empire in the West, or of the decline of the Oriental Caliphate in the Middle East.

Rather than seeing their inter-relation as a mechanical correspondence, it is *the dialectic between productive forces and social relations of production* which to a large extent determines the succession of great epochs in human history. Each mode of production passes through the successive phases of birth, growth, maturity, decline, fall, and disappearance. In the final analysis, these phases depend on the manner in which the relations of production, initially new, then consolidated, then in crisis, progressively favour, allow or hinder the growth of the productive forces. The articulation between this dialectic and the class struggle is evident. It is only through the action of a social class or several social classes that a given set of relations of production can be introduced, conserved or overthrown.

Every social formation, that is, every society in a given country, in a given epoch, is always characterised by a totality of relations of production. A social formation without relations of production would be a country without labour, production, or subsistence — that is, a country without inhabitants. But every totality of social relations of production does not necessarily imply the existence of a stabilized mode of production, nor the homogeneity of these relations of production.

A stabilised mode of production is a totality of relations of production which are reproduced more or less automatically by the actual functioning of the economy, by the normal pattern of reproduction of the productive forces, with a correlative role (more or less important) of certain factors of the social superstructure. This was the case for centuries in many countries of the Asiatic, slave, feudal, and capitalist modes of production. This was the case for thousands of years with the tribal communist mode of production. In this sense, a mode of production is a structure which cannot be fundamentally modified by evolution, adaptation or self-reform. Its internal logic can only be transcended if it is overthrown.

On the contrary, in periods of profound historical social upheaval, one can experience a sum total of relations of production which do not have the nature of a stabilised mode of production. A typical example is that of the epoch when petty commodity production predominated (the Fifteenth and Sixteenth Centuries in the Low Countries, in North Italy, and then in England), in which the prevailing relations were not those between lords and serfs, nor between capitalists and wage-earning producers, but those of free producers having direct access to their means of production. It is the same for the characteristic relations of production in today's bureaucratised workers states. Neither in one case nor the other can one demonstrate the existence of a stabilised mode of production. In all these *societies in a transitional phase* the hybrid relations of production are not structures which reproduce themselves more or less automatically. They can lead either to the restoration of the old society or to the arrival of a new mode of production. This historic alternative is governed by a number of factors, mainly the sufficient or insufficient growth of the productive forces, the result of the class struggle in a given country and on an international scale, the play of superstructural and subjective elements (role of the state, of the party, level of combativity and consciousness of the revolutionary class, etc.).

On the other hand, even when a stabilised mode of production exists, the relations of production are not necessarily homogeneous. They hardly ever are. In every concrete social formation there is always a *combination* between the predominant relations of production of the existing mode of production and the not entirely absorbed vestiges of previous relations of production which were historically transcended a long time ago. For example, practically all the imperialist countries still contain some vestiges of petty commodity production in agriculture (small peasant owners, working without wage-earning labour) and even vestiges of semi-feudal relations of production (share-cropping). In these cases it is correct to talk of a stabilised mode of production when the predominance of the relations of production characteristic of it is such that it assures their automatic reproduction and their domination over the whole of economic life through their internal logic and laws of development.

A characteristic example of hybrid relations of production dominated by a hegemonic mode of production is that of so-called 'third world' social formations (for under-developed countries see Chapter 7). Here pre-capitalist, semi-capitalist and capitalist relations of production exist side by side, *combined in a determined manner* under the pressure of the international economy's imperialist structure. In spite of the predominance of capital, and in spite of insertion into the imperialist system, capitalist relations of production (above all, the 'wage labour-capital' relation) do not become generalised, although they exist and slowly extend. But this fact hardly justifies the characterisation of these social formations as 'feudal countries', nor the contention that feudal or semi-feudal relations of production predominate within them, a theoretical error committed by many social democratic, Stalinist and Maoist theoreticians.

5 Historical determinism and revolutionary practice

Historical materialism is a determinist doctrine. Its fundamental thesis affirms that it is social existence which determines social consciousness. The history of human societies can be explained. Its course is not haphazard or arbitrary. Its unfolding does not depend on unforeseeable whims of genetic mutation, or 'great men' among the atomised multitude. In the last analysis it is explained by the fundamental structure of the society at each given epoch, and by the essential contradictions of this structure. For as long as society is divided into classes, it is explained by class struggle.

But if historical materialism is a determinist doctrine, this is so in the dialectical and not the mechanistic sense of the term. Marxism excludes fatalism. More precisely: any attempt to transform Marxism into automatic fatalism or vulgar evolutionism eliminates a fundamental dimension of it.

While it is true of course that humanity's choices are predetermined by material and social constraints from which it cannot escape, it can forge its own destiny within the framework of these constraints. Humanity makes its own history. If humanity is the product of given material conditions, these material conditions are in turn the products of *human social practice*.

This transcending of old historical idealism ('ideas, or great men, make history') and of old mechanical materialism ('people are the product of circumstances') is in a way the birth of Marxism. It is contained in the famous 'Theses on Feuerbach' which conclude *The German Ideology* by Marx and Engels.

Among other things, this signifies that the result of each great epoch of social convulsions in history remains uncertain. It can lead to the victory of the revolutionary class. It can also lead to the reciprocal decomposition of all the fundamental classes of a given society, as was the case at the end of the ancient mode of production based on slavery. History is not the sum total of linear progressions. Many past social formations have disappeared without leaving many traces, mainly through the absence or weakness of a revolutionary class capable of forging a way towards progress.

The evident decadence of contemporary capitalism does not automatically lead to the victory of socialism. It leads to the alternative 'socialism or barbarism'. Socialism is a historical necessity to permit a new upsurge in the productive forces which is consistent with the possibilities of contemporary science and technology. It is above all a human necessity, in that it will permit the satisfaction of needs, in conditions that assure the blossoming of all human potential in all individuals and all peoples, without destroying the ecological balance. But what is necessary is not necessarily what is achieved. Only the revolutionary and conscious action of the proletariat can guarantee the triumph of socialism. Otherwise the enormous productive potential of contemporary science and technology will assume a progressively more destructive form as regards civilisation, culture, humanity, nature, and, quite simply, life on our planet.

It is humanity's social practice that creates the social structures which subsequently envelop it. Through revolutionary social practice these same structures can be overthrown. Marxism is determinist in that it affirms that these upheavals can only take certain forms in certain epochs. It is impossible to reintroduce feudalism, or the communism of small autarchic communities of producer-consumers, on the basis of contemporary productive forces. It is determinist in that it stresses that progressive social revolutions are only possible if the material preconditions and social forces which permit the creation of a superior social organisation have already matured within the old society.

But Marxism is not fatalistic, because in no way does it postulate that the arrival of this new society is the inevitable product of the ripening of the material and social conditions necessary for its appearance. This arrival can only result from the outcome of struggles between living social forces. In the last analysis, it results from the *degree of social effectiveness of revolutionary action.* If this is in turn partially conditioned by social circumstances and the balance of forces, revolutionary action can overturn, brake or accelerate the evolution of these circumstances and balance of forces. Even an eminently favourable balance of forces can be 'spoilt' by subjective deficiencies on the part of the revolutionary class. In this sense, in our epoch of revolution and counter-revolution, the 'subjective factor of history' (the class consciousness and revolutionary leadership of the proletariat) plays a primordial role in determining the result of great class battles, in deciding the future of the human species.

6 Alienation and emancipation

For thousands of years humanity lived in strict dependence on the uncontrollable forces of nature. It could only try to adapt to a given natural milieu, each little human group to its own. It was the prisoner of a narrow and constricted horizon, even if several primitive societies were able to develop certain human potentialities in a remarkable manner (for example, paleolithic painting).

Within the gradual development of the productive forces, humanity manages little by little to overturn this relationship of absolute dependence. It succeeds in subjugating the forces of nature more and more, in controlling them, domesticating them, using them consciously in order to increase production, to diversify needs, to develop human potentialities, and to extend social relations so as finally to encompass and partially unify humanity on a world scale.

But the more people emancipate themselves in relation to the forces of nature, the more they alienate themselves in relation to their own social organisation. As the productive forces grow, as material production progresses, as relations of production become those of a society divided into classes, the mass of humanity no longer controls the entirety of its production or the whole of its productive activity. It therefore no longer controls its social existence. In capitalist society this loss of control becomes total. Freed from subjection to the whims of nature, humanity seems fated to

186

become subject to the whims of its own social organisation. Freed from the irresistible effects of floods, earthquakes, epidemics and droughts, it appears to be condemned instead to the effects of war and economic crises, bloody dictatorships and the criminal destruction of the productive forces, even the possibility of nuclear destruction. The fear of these cataclysms inspires even more anxiety today than the fear of hunger, illness or death did before.

However, the same impressive development of the productive forces which pushes the alienation of humanity to the limit in relation to its own production and its own society also creates, under capitalism, the possibility for a real emancipation of humanity, as we have already indicated at the end of Chapter 2. This possibility must be understood in a dual sense. More and more, humanity will be capable of controlling and determining its social development as well as the upheavals in the natural milieu in which this takes place. Humanity will be increasingly capable of developing to the full all its potentialities of individual and social development, previously stifled or mutilated by its insufficient control over the forces of nature, social organisation, and its own social destiny.

The construction of a classless society, and then the coming of a communist society, implies the emancipation of labour, the emancipation of humanity as producer. The workers become masters of their products and processes of work. They freely choose the priorities in the division of the social product. They decide collectively and democratically the order in which needs are to be fulfilled, the productive priorities, the sacrifices of leisure-time and current consumption which this allocation of resources will imply.

Of course, these choices will continue to be made within a certain framework of constraint. No human society can consume more than it produces without reducing its reserves and productive resources and condemning itself to a reduction in current consumption at a later date, when the draining of reserves and the reduction of productive resources has reached a certain threshold. In this sense, Frederick Engels' formula stating that freedom is the recognition of necessity remains true even for communist humanity. 'The taking in hand of necessity' would be more correct than 'recognition', as the more humanity's control over its natural and social conditions of existence grows, the more the number of possible responses to constraining conditions grow, and the more humanity can emancipate itself from the obligation to adopt just one response.

But there is a second dimension to human disalienation, which greatly enlarges the sphere of human liberty. When all basic needs of all people are satisfied, when the reproduction of this abundance is assured, the solving of material problems ceases to be a priority for humanity. Humanity emancipates itself from enslavement to mechanistic, un-creative labour. It liberates itself from the niggardly measurement of how it uses its time and from the devotion of that time mainly to material production. The development of creative activities, the development of humanity's rich individuality, the development of wider and wider human relations all take priority over the constant accumulation of material goods which are less and less useful.

Thenceforth revolutionary social practice will not only overthrow relations of production. It will change all social organisation, all the traditional customs, mentality and psychology of humanity. Material egoism and the aggressive competitive spirit will fade away for lack of nourishment in daily experience.

Humanity will master its geographical surroundings, the configuration of the globe, the climate and the distribution of great water reserves, at the same time preserving or re-establishing ecological equilibrium. It will overturn everything down to its own biological foundations. It cannot achieve these objectives in an absolutely voluntarist manner, independent of preconditions and a sufficient material infrastructure. But once this infrastructure is assured, it is active humanity, more and more free in its choices, which will become the principal lever for the creation of the new person, the free and disalienated communist. It is in this sense that it is correct to talk of communist and Marxist humanism.

Further Reading

This Bibliography has been compiled using the 1976 volumes of American and British Books in Print. Some titles may have since gone out of print; others, at the time not available in English, may have since been translated. The titles by Marx and Engels either are or will become available in the Lawrence and Wishart 50 volume Complete Works. Similarly, any of Lenin's writings referred to can be found in the Complete Works (Progress Publishers, Moscow), and most of them in the three volume Selected Works. On the other hand, almost all the works by Marx, Engels and Lenin cited below are available as individual pamphlets or books, or occasionally in anthologies. And as these are both handier and cheaper to use we have referred the reader to these editions. Where no reference is made to a publisher, or where the title is in a foreign language, the book has not been translated to our knowledge or, at least, has no current edition available in English.

Chapter One

Marx and Engels: *The Communist Manifesto* [Intro. by L. Trotsky] (Pathfinder Press, N.Y., '73).

Engels: *Anti-Dühring* [second and third parts] (Lawrence and Wishart, London '75).

Max Beer: *Histoire du Socialisme*.

Karl Kautsky: *Foundations of Christianity* (Orbach and Chambers '73; Monthly Review, US, '72).

A.L. Morton: *The English Utopia* (Lawrence and Wishart, London, '69).

Karl Kautsky: *Thomas More and his Utopia* (Russell, US, '59).

Chapter Two

Marx and Engels: *The Communist Manifesto* (see above).

Engels: *Anti-Dühring* [second and third parts] (see above).

Gordon V. Childe: *What Happened in History* (Penguin, London, '69).

: *Man Makes Himself* (Fontana, London, '66).

G. Glotz: *Ancient Greece at Work* (Norton, US, '67).

Boisonnade: *Le Travail au Moyen-âge*.

E. Mandel: *Marxist Economic Theory* [first four chapters] (Merlin Pr., London, '72).

Chapter Three

Marx and Engels: *The Communist Manifesto* (see above).

Engels: *Origin of the Family, Private Property and the State* (Pathfinder Pr., N.Y., '72).

Herman Gorter: *Het historisch materialisme*.

N. Bukharin: *Historical Materialism* (Ann Arbor, US, '69).

George Plekhanov: *Fundamental Questions of Marxism* (Lawrence and Wishart, London, '69).

K. Kautsky: *L'Ethique et la Concéption Matérialiste de l'Histoire*.

A. Moret and G. Davy: *From Tribe to Empire* (Cooper Sq., US, '71).

Chapter Four

K. Marx: *Wages, Price and Profit* (Progress, Moscow).
Rosa Luxemburg: *Introduction à L'Economie Politique*.
E. Mandel: *Introduction to Marxist Economic Theory* (Pathfinder, N.Y., '73).
E. Mandel: *Marxist Economic Theory* (see above).
Pierre Salama and Jacques Valier: *Introduction à L'Economie Politique* (Maspéro, Paris).

Chapter Five

K. Marx: *Wages, Price and Profit* (see above).
K. Marx and F. Engels: *The Communist Manifesto* (see above).
F. Engels: *Anti-Dühring* [second part] (see above).
K. Kautsky: *The Economic Doctrine of Karl Marx*.
R. Luxemburg: *Introduction à L'Economie Politique*.
E. Mandel: *Introduction to Marxist Economic Theory* (see above).
P. Salama and J. Valier: *Introduction à l'Economie Politique* (see above).
E. Mandel: *Marxist Economic Theory* (see above).
E. Mandel and George Novack: *The Marxist Theory of Alienation* (Pathfinder, N.Y., '73).

Chapter Six

Lenin: *Imperialism, the Highest Stage of Capitalism* (Progress, Moscow).
R. Hilferding: *Finance Capital*.
E. Mandel: *Marxist Economic Theory* (see above).
Pierre Jalée: *Imperialism in the Seventies* (Third World Press, US, '73).
P. Salama: *Le Procès de Sous-Développement* (Critique de L'Economie Politique, Maspéro, Paris).

Chapter Seven

P. Jalée: *Imperialism in the Seventies* (see above).
P. Salama: *Le Procès de Sous-Développement* (see above).
Paul A. Baran: *The Political Economy of Growth* (Monthly Review, US, '57).
Haupt-Lowy-Weill: *Les Marxistes et la question nationale* [texts from Lenin, Luxemburg, Otto Bauer, etc.] (Maspéro, Paris).
Michael Barratt-Brown: *After Imperialism* (Heinemann, London, '63).
Leon Trotsky: *Permanent Revolution* (Pathfinder, US).
              : *The Third International After Lenin* (Pathfinder).
Lenin: *Imperialism, the Highest Stage of Capitalism* (see above).
R. Luxemburg: *The Accumulation of Capital* [last six chapters] (Monthly Review, US, '64).
N. Bukharin: *Imperialism and the World Economy* (Merlin, London, '72).

Chapter Eight

Marx and Engels: *The Communist Manifesto* (see above).
F. Engels: *Socialism: Utopian and Scientific* (Pathfinder, N.Y., '72).

Max Beer: *Histoire du Socialisme.*

K. Marx: *The Civil War in France* [Collection 'On the Paris Commune'] (Progress, Moscow, '71).

Prosper Lissagaray: *History of the Paris Commune of 1871* (New Park, London, '76).

A.L. Morton and G. Tate: *The British Labour Movement 1770-1920* (Lawrence and Wishart, London, '74).

Wolfgang Abendroth: *A Short History of the European Working Class* (NLB, London, '72).

E.P. Thompson: *The Making of the English Working Class* (Penguin, London, '70).

Chapter Nine

Lenin: *What Is To Be Done?* (Foreign Language Press, Peking, '73).
    : *Left Wing Communism, an Infantile Disorder* (Progress, Moscow).
R. Luxemburg: *Reform or Revolution* (Pathfinder, N.Y., '75, Ed. Waters, M-A).

        : *The Mass Strike* (as above).

Chapter Ten

K. Marx: *The Civil War in France* (see above).
Lenin: *State and Revolution* (Progress, Moscow).
    : *The Proletarian Revolution and the Renegade Kautsky* (Foreign Language Pr., Peking, '70).
L. Trotsky: *The Struggle Against Fascism in Germany* (Pelican, London, '75).
Fifth Congress of the Fourth International (F.I.): *Theses on the Decline and Fall of Stalinism* (Education for Socialists, Socialist Workers Party (SWP), '70).

Chapter Eleven

Lenin: *Two Tactics of Social Democracy* (Progress, Moscow).
    : *The Impending Catastrophe and How to Fight It* (as above).
    : *Can the Bolsheviks Retain State Power?* (as above).
R. Luxemburg: *The Junius Pamphlet* (Pathfinder, N.Y., '75, Ed. Waters, M-A).

        : *The Russian Revolution and Leninism or Marxism* (as above).
L. Trotsky: *Permanent Revolution* (see above).
        : *History of the Russian Revolution* (Pluto, London, '77).
        : *Three Conceptions of the Russian Revolution* [Appendix to 'Stalin', vol. 2] (Panther, London, '69).
        : *Copenhagen Speeches* [*1932*] (New Park, London, '71).

Chapter Twelve

E. Mandel: *On Bureaucracy* (IMG Publications, '73).
L. Trotsky: *The Lessons of October; the New Course, 1923* [The Challenge of the Left Opposition 1923-25, Ed. Allen, N.] (Pathfinder, N.Y., '75).

: *The Revolution Betrayed* (Pathfinder, N.Y.).
Moshe Lewin: *Lenin's Last Struggle* (Pluto, London, '75).
Theses of the Fourth and Fifth Congresses of the F.I.: *Rise and Decline of Stalinism; Decline and Disintegration of Stalinism* (Education for Socialists, SWP, '70).
Samizdat, Voices from the Opposition (Pathfinder, N.Y., '74).
Bill Lomax: *Hungary 1956* (Motive, Allison and Busby, London, '76).

Chapter Thirteen

L. Trotsky: *The Transitional Programme* (Pathfinder, N.Y., '74).
Seventh World Congress of the F.I. (Congress of Reunification): *Dynamics of World Revolution Today* (International Socialist Review, '63).
E. Mandel: *Workers Control* (International, Vol. 2 No. 1, Spring '73).
E. Mandel: *Workers Control, Workers Councils, Self-Management* (anthology, Maspéro, Paris).
E. Mandel: *Why the Fourth International?* (IMG Pubs., London).
Documents of the Ninth and Tenth World Congresses of the F.I. (Intercontinental Press, N.Y., July '69, & Dec. '74).

Chapter Fourteen

Resolution of the Third Congress of the Communist International on Tactics (Ink Links, London, '78).
Lenin: *Left Wing Communism, an Infantile Disorder* (see above).
L. Trotsky: *Whither France?* (Pathfinder, N.Y.).
: *Struggle Against Fascism in Germany* (see above). [See Mandel's introduction to this volume: *On Fascism.*]
: *Writings on Spain* (Pathfinder, N.Y.).
Daniel Guérin: *Fascism and Big Business* (Monad, N.Y., '73).
Henri Weber: *Marxism and Class Consciousness* (10:18, Paris, '76).
E. Mandel: *Leninist Theory of Organisation* (in 'Revolution and Class Struggle: A Reader in Marxist Politics', Fontana, London, Ed. Blackburn, R., '77).

Chapter Fifteen

K. Marx: *Critique of the Gotha Programme* (Progress, Moscow).
F. Engels: *Anti-Dühring* [part three: Socialism] (see above).
Lenin: *State and Revolution* (see above).
Bukharin and E. Preobrazhensky: *ABC of Communism* (Penguin, London, '69).
L. Trotsky: *Literature and Revolution* (Ann Arbor, No. 43, U.S.).
: *Problems of Everyday Life* (Pathfinder, N.Y.).
Paul Lafargue: *The Right to be Lazy* (Charles H. Kerr, Chicago, '75).

Chapter Sixteen

N. Bukharin: *Historical Materialism* (see above).
F. Engels: *Anti-Dühring* [part 4] (see above).
: *Ludwig Feuerbach and the End of Classical German Philosophy*

(Fontana, Marx and Engels anthology, Ed. Feuer, London, '69).

Henri Lefebvre: *Dialectical Materialism* (Cape, London, '68).

Lenin: *Writings on Dialectics* [Philosophical Notebooks] (Progress, Moscow).

G. Novack: *An Introduction to the Logic of Marxism* (Pathfinder, N.Y.).

G. Lukàcs: *History and Class Consciousness* [first two chapters] (Merlin, London, '71).

G. Plekhanov: *Fundamental Questions of Marxism* (see above).

Chapter Seventeen

N. Bukharin: *Historical Materialism* (see above).

F. Engels: *Ludwig Feuerbach and the End of Classical German Philosophy* (see above)

      : *Socialism, Utopian and Scientific* (see above).

      : *The Part Played by Labour in the Transition from Ape to Man.*

Antonio Gramsci: *Historical Materialism* [extracts from the *Prison Notebooks*] (Lawrence and Wishart, London, '71).

K. Kautsky: *L'Ethique et la Concéption Materialiste d'Histoire.*

G. Lukàcs: *Criticism of N. Bukharin's manual of sociology* (L'Homme et la Société, No. 2, '66).

E. Mandel: *The Formation of the Economic Thought of Karl Marx* [last two chapters] (NLB, London, '75).

K. Marx: *Preface to the 'Contribution to a Critique of Political Economy'* (Pluto, London, '71).

Marx and Engels: *The German Ideology* (Lawrence and Wishart, London, '74).

Franz Mehring: *Essays on Historical Materialism* (New Park, London, '75).

G. Plekhanov: *Art and Social Life* (Lawrence and Wishart, London, '74).

Tran-Duc-Thau: *On the Birth of Consciousness and Language.*

Unsolved Mysteries

Giant Humanlike Beasts

Brian Innes

RSVP
RAINTREE
STECK-VAUGHN
P U B L I S H E R S
A Steck-Vaughn Company

Austin, Texas

Developed by Brown Partworks

Editor: Lindsey Lowe
Designer: Joan Curtis
Picture Researcher: Brigitte Arora

Raintree Steck-Vaughn Publishers Staff

Project Manager: Joyce Spicer
Editor: Pam Wells

Library of Congress Cataloging-in-Publication Data

Innes, Brian.
Giant humanlike beasts/by Brian Innes.
p.   cm.—(Unsolved mysteries)
Includes bibliographical references and index.
ISBN 0-8172-5484-6 (Hardcover)
ISBN 0-8172-5846-9 (Softcover)
1. Yeti—Juvenile literature. 2. Sasquatch—Juvenile literature.
3. Wild men—Juvenile literature.
I. Title. II. Series: Innes, Brian. Unsolved mysteries.
QL89.2.Y4I56   1999
001.944—dc21   98-28736
                                                  CIP
                                                  AC

Printed and bound in the United States
1 2 3 4 5 6 7 8 9 0   WZ   02 01 00 99 98

Acknowledgments

Cover Galen Rowell/Corbis; **Page 5:** Christine
Kolisch/Corbis; **Page 6:** Ivan T. Sanderson/Fortean
Picture Library; **Page 7:** Keren Su/Corbis; **Page 9:**
Eric Shipton and Michael Ward/Mary Evans Picture
Library; **Page 10:** John Cleare; **Page 11:** Hulton-
Deutsch Collection/Corbis; **Page 13:** Michael S.
Yamashita/Corbis; **Page 14:** Fortean Picture Library;
Page 15: Dr. Zhou Guoxing/Fortean Picture Library;
Page 16: International Society of Cryptozoology;
Page 17: Natural History Museum, London; **Page 19:**
Bridgeman Art Library; **Page 20:** George Lepp/Corbis;
Page 21: Keren Su/Corbis; **Page 23:** Rene Dahinden
/Fortean Picture Library; **Page 24:** UPI/Corbis-
Bettmann; **Page 25:** Fortean Picture Library;
Page 27: Patterson/Gimlin © 1968, Rene
Dahinden/Fortean Picture Library; **Page 28:** Fortean
Picture Library; **Page 29:** Gunter Marx/Corbis;
Pages 30, 32, 33, 34: Rene Dahinden/Fortean Picture
Library; **Page 35:** Popperfoto; **Page 37:** Loren
Coleman/Fortean Picture Library; **Page 38:** Fortean
Picture Library; **Page 41:** Natural History Museum,
London; **Page 43:** Wolfgang Kaehler/Corbis;
Page 44: Popperfoto; **Page 45:** Fortean Picture
Library; **Page 46:** Cliff Crook/Fortean Picture Library.

9229

Contents

Abominable Snowman

Somewhere in the cold Himalaya Mountains lives a giant beast. It is known as the Abominable Snowman.

The Himalaya Mountains stretch for more than 1,500 miles (2,413.5 km) along the northern border of India. In spring, 1925, photographer N. A. Tombazi was with a group of climbers in the Himalayas. They had reached the Zemu Glacier, at a height of 15,000 feet (4,575 m). Apart from a few small bushes, snow stretched all around them. Suddenly one of the local guides stopped. He pointed to a spot about 300 yards (274 m) away.

At first Tombazi could see nothing. He was blinded by the sun shining off the snow. Then he spotted a figure. It was walking upright, stopping every now and then to pull at the bushes. Tombazi said: "It showed up dark against the snow and, as far as I could make out, wore no clothes. Within the next minute or so it had moved into some thick scrub. . . ." It could not be seen in the bushes and shrubs.

"A couple of hours later, I purposely made a detour [changed direction], so as to pass the place where the 'man' or 'beast' had been seen. I examined the footprints, which were clearly visible on the surface of the snow. They were similar in shape to those of a man."

Every year, groups of climbers and their local guides begin to climb the mountains of the Himalayas (opposite). Many have found mysterious trails of footprints in the smooth, white snow.

4

People call the Himalaya Mountains "the roof of the world." The highest point is Mount Everest. . . .

Tombazi was a member of the British Royal Geographical Society. This is a scientific organization that is respected worldwide. He was certainly somebody to be trusted. He had no doubt that he had seen the creature known locally as the "yeti."

HOME OF THE YETI

People call the Himalaya Mountains "the roof of the world." At 15,000 feet (4,575 m), there is snow all year round—the word "Himalaya" actually means "home of the snows." There are some 96 peaks at a height of over 24,000 feet (7,320 m), but the highest point is Mount Everest, at 29,028 feet (8,848 m).

Mount Everest stands right on the border between China and Nepal. Nepal is a small country in the Himalayas that lies between northern India and China. The people who live on the lower slopes of Mount Everest are called Sherpas. They believe that there are two kinds of creatures living among the high snows. The Sherpas call one of them *dzu-teh*. Experts think that this is probably the common Himalayan black bear. The other is the *yeh-teh*, or yeti.

The Sherpas describe the yeti as being about the size of a human. They say it has a pointed head and walks upright on two legs. It has long arms and is covered with reddish hair. The yeti is said to live in the area where the trees stop and the high snows begin. Sometimes it

This is a drawing of what a Himalayan yeti, or "snowman," might look like.

6

This Tibetan farmer is using a couple of yaks to pull his plow. Some farmers have reported that their yaks have been killed by yetis in search of food.

moves down the mountainside to steal food from villages. It may also kill yaks—large, hairy oxen that the farmers keep for milk, plowing, and clothing.

The first report of a yeti sighting by a European came from a British major, L. A. Waddell, in 1889. He found large humanlike footprints in the snow while climbing on Everest at a height of 17,000 feet (5,185 m). He wrote that some claimed these prints were "the trail of the hairy wild man believed to live among the eternal [everlasting] snows." But Waddell decided that they were likely to be the tracks of a bear. For more than 30 years, nobody paid much attention to his report. Then the yeti gained a new name that made it world famous.

HUNT FOR THE SNOWMAN

In 1921 a man named Kenneth Howard-Bury was leading a British expedition to Mount Everest. At around 20,000 feet (6,100 m), he and his team saw dark figures moving across the snow above them. When they reached the spot, they found a series of giant footprints. The Sherpa guides said they must have been made by *metoh-kangmi*. This was a term or nickname that the Sherpas used to describe any unknown mountain animal. When Howard-Bury reported his sighting, the nickname was translated, or put into English, as the "Abominable Snowman."

A huge yeti, nearly 9 feet (3 m) tall, picked him up and carried him to a cave.

The name caught the attention of newspaper editors all over the world. At the time, there were many mountaineers, or people who climb mountains, who wanted to be the first to reach the very top of Mount Everest. Now they had an additional purpose—to find the Abominable Snowman.

TALL TALES?

In 1938, Captain d'Auvergne told an amazing story. He said he had been traveling alone in the Himalayas. He was exhausted and nearly blinded by the snow. A huge yeti, nearly 9 feet (3 m) tall, picked him up and carried him to a cave. There the creature fed and looked after him until he was able to walk again.

The next sighting was made in 1942. Slavomir Rawicz was a Pole. He had been captured by the Russians during World War II, but he and six others had escaped from their prison camp. They had walked 2,000 miles (3,218 km) to freedom, crossing the Himalayas into India. On the way they met two huge yeti: "They were nearly 8 feet [2.5 m] tall . . . The heads were squarish [square-shaped]. The shoulders sloped sharply down to a powerful chest and long arms, the wrists of which reached the knees."

Rawicz said he and his companions watched the creatures for two hours. One was slightly larger than the other, and Rawicz guessed they were male and female. They did not seem interested in the humans.

In 1951, British climbers Eric Shipton and Michael Ward were walking on Mount Everest when they found a set of tracks. They followed them for nearly a mile. One footprint was very clear. They took photographs of it. Ward put his ice ax beside it to give an idea of the size. This proved the footprint was nearly 13 inches (33 cm) long and 8 inches (20 cm) wide.

This is a photograph of one of the footprints that Eric Shipton and Michael Ward found in the Himalayas in 1951. The print was 13 inches (33 cm) long.

This Tibetan man is holding what was said to be the scalp of a yeti. However, an expert said it was made from goat skin.

Describing his experience later, Eric Shipton wrote: "There could be no doubt whatever that a large creature had passed that way a very short time before. Whatever it was, it was not a human being, not a bear, not any species of monkey known to exist in Asia." The footprint had five toes. The two inner toes were longer than the rest. The heel was very broad and flat.

The photographs were looked at by a group of scientists who study animals. They said that they thought the tracks might have been made by a bear, or by some type of large monkey. Nevertheless Shipton, and many other people, refused to believe the prints had been made by animals.

ON TOP OF THE WORLD

Two years later New Zealander Edmund Hillary and Sherpa Tenzing Norgay were the first men to stand on the top of Mount Everest. But the news of their success was almost forgotten when they reported that they, too, had seen the tracks of the yeti. Tenzing said he had often seen similar tracks. He told Hillary that his father had once been chased down a steep slope by one of the creatures.

A London newspaper, the *Daily Mail*, organized its own Abominable Snowman Expedition in 1954. It had little success, however. A reporter named Ralph Izzard led the expedition. The team only found a few tracks in the snow. They also photographed what was said to be the scalp of a yeti, which they found in a Tibetan monastery. A monastery is a building where monks live. In 1961, Edmund Hillary borrowed the scalp and took it to be examined by experts. They announced that it was made from the skin of a wild goat that lived in the area!

Many people have seen Abominable Snowman footprints like these in the snows of the Himalayas. Some have photographed them. However, nobody has yet photographed the creature itself—if it exists!

THE MYSTERY LIVES ON

In recent years, after the excitement of the 1950s, less has been heard about the Abominable Snowman. However, reports are still being made today. Some unknown creature surely exists high in the Himalaya Mountains, leaving footprints in the snow and scaring the local Sherpas.

Interestingly, reports of such a creature do not come only from this area. There are also stories of the Wildman deep in the forests of China; creatures called the Almas in central Asia; the Bigfoot in North America; and many other strange humanlike beasts.

Wildman of China

There are many tales of a large, humanlike creature living in the wild forests of the Chinese mountains.

The valley of the Chang (Yangtze) River is bordered by thick forests (opposite). Most of these are unexplored. Many people think they are home to the Wildman of China.

One evening early in 1976, some Chinese loggers were traveling in their truck down a dirt road through the forest. They had been working high in the mountains of Hubei Province. This is a wild area 600 miles (965 km) up the valley of the great Chang (Yangtze) River. There are huge, thick forests, almost unexplored, and few roads or villages.

Suddenly the headlights of the truck showed a large, hairy figure. It was standing in the middle of the dirt road. The driver braked quickly, and several men got down. They approached to within just a few yards of the creature. Then it turned and disappeared into the undergrowth.

A CHINESE LEGEND

The men were sure it was not a bear. And it was not any other forest animal they had seen before. They decided that it must have been a "Wildman." Tales of the Wildman have been told by the Chinese for many centuries. Like the Abominable Snowman of the Himalaya Mountains, the Wildman is said to be tall, heavily built, and covered with hair. The men sent a report to the Chinese Academy of Sciences.

The men were sure it was not a bear. . . . They decided that it must have been a "Wildman."

For a long time experts did not believe these stories. But then, in 1950, a scientist named Fan Jingquan reported that he had sighted two creatures in a forest in Shanxi Province.

Other sightings began to be reported. In 1961, men were building a road through a thick forest in the Yunnan Province. They claimed that they had killed a young female Wildman. They said that it was only about 4 feet (1.2 m) tall. The Chinese Academy of Sciences immediately sent a team of experts to the area, but they could find no trace of the body. They decided it must have been a monkey.

The Wildman is said to be large and covered with thick hair, as shown in the drawing on this Chinese poster. The writing says, "Have you seen the Wildman?"

COLLECTING PROOF

After the 1976 sighting in Hubei Province, there were many more reports, all from the same region, or area. The Chinese government decided to see if they could find any proof that the creature existed. A scientific team was put together by Zhou Guoxing, a professor at the Natural History Museum in Beijing. There were nearly 100 experts in the group. They were helped by several units from the Chinese Army.

Over a period of two years, the scientific team carefully searched through the thick forests of Hubei Province. They covered an area of some 500 square miles (1,295 sq km) and gathered dozens of descriptions from local people.

One report was particularly interesting. In June 1976, a woman named Gong Yulan said that she had seen a hairy, humanlike creature. It was scratching its back against a tree. She showed the scientists the tree, and they found hairs trapped in the bark. The hairs were sent back to be examined in Beijing. Experts reported that they came from an unknown animal. It was an apelike creature. But the hairs did not match those from any known species.

FACE-TO-FACE

The most amazing story was told by Pang Gensheng. He was a team leader from a local commune, or rural community. He said that he had been out chopping wood when he met a Wildman.

The creature had walked toward him. Terrified, Gensheng backed away until he found himself up against the bottom of a cliff. He had nowhere to go. The Wildman approached. Gensheng raised his ax to

Gong Yulan (at center) talking to Dr. Zhou Guoxing and a group of Chinese soldiers. She claimed to have seen a Wildman by this tree on June 19, 1976.

15

protect himself, and the creature stopped. Gensheng said he and the Wildman stood looking at each other for nearly an hour. Then he reached down and picked up a large rock. He threw it and hit the beast in the chest. It howled and then ran a short distance away. Afterward it stopped and leaned against a tree before running off. Gensheng said the Wildman had been about 7 feet (2 m) tall. He said it had wide shoulders, a sloping forehead, and long arms.

These were just two reports of the sightings in Hubei Province. The members of the scientific expedition were very excited. But they were unable to spot a Wildman for themselves. However, they did find huge footprints and several individual hairs.

GIANT APES

Dr. Guoxing was just one of many scientists who were convinced that the animal existed. In 1980 he was sent some preserved hands and feet. They were said to have been taken from a dead Wildman. However, when Guoxing looked at them carefully, he decided that they came from a type of monkey. This could explain the small "Wildman" killed by the road builders in Yunnan Province.

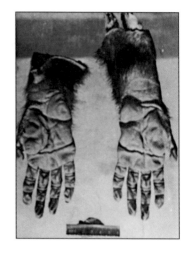

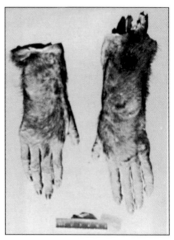

Dr. Guoxing photographed the "Wildman hands" sent to him in 1980 (top and above). The 6-inch (15 cm) rule shows their size.

As an expert on prehistoric beings, Guoxing knew all about the large *Gigantopithecus* ape species that has died out. In 1935 a German scientist, G. H. R. von

Koenigswald, had bought some large teeth from a Chinese druggist in Hong Kong. Koenigswald was an anthropologist, an expert on the beginnings, development, and customs of humans. He believed that the teeth were from a huge, humanlike creature.

Twenty years later a Chinese anthropologist, Pei Wen Xung, proved that they had, in fact, come from a huge ape that had lived in China until about a million years ago. Because of its size the creature was called *Gigantopithecus*, meaning "giant ape." It was said to be bigger than a large gorilla—around 12 feet (4 m) tall and close to 690 pounds (313 kg). Dr. Guoxing wondered if these apes could still be living in China after all. He pointed out that other ancient species are still with us today. These include the tapir, which is a large animal with hoofs that looks something like a pig, and the giant panda. Both species of animals are found in China.

A LIVING WILDMAN?

There are still many creatures to be discovered in the unexplored parts of the world. Does *Gigantopithecus* still live deep in the Chinese forests? Or perhaps the Wildman is an even closer but unknown relative of modern humans.

This drawing shows an adult Gigantopithecus and its baby. Perhaps this creature is the real "Wildman" of China.

17

The Asian Almas

The lands of central Asia cover a large area of the world. It is possible that wild people roam its most distant parts.

Early in the 15th century, Hans Schiltberger, a Bavarian soldier from southern Germany, was captured by the Turks. He was treated as a slave, and after a while was sold to a Mongol prince. The prince's name was Timur (Tamerlane), and although Schiltberger was still a slave, he became one of the prince's advisors. Working for Prince Timur, Schiltberger traveled throughout central Asia. However, he finally managed to escape and find his way back home to Europe.

A GREAT ADVENTURE

In 1430, Schiltberger wrote an account of his adventures. He described some of the many wild creatures that he had seen on his travels through Asia: "In the mountains live wild people who have nothing in common with other humans. Only the hands and face are free of hair. They run around in the hills like animals, and eat foliage [the leaves of a tree or plant] and grass, and whatever else they can find. The lord of the territory made . . . a present of a couple of forest people, a man and a woman. They had been caught in the wilderness, together with three untamed horses. . . ."

This picture shows Prince Timur with some of his advisors (opposite). While working for the prince, Schiltberger saw many amazing people and animals.

Working for Prince Timur, Schiltberger traveled throughout central Asia.

A female Przewalski's horse and her foal. Very few survive in their native Mongolia. These horses were photographed in a wildlife park in California.

More than four centuries later, in the 1870s, the Russian explorer Nikolai Przewalski discovered these wild Mongolian horses. The species has been named after him. It is now extremely rare, although a few horses are protected in wildlife parks. On the same expedition Przewalski also heard tales of "wild men," but unfortunately he was unable to discover any.

ANIMAL OR HUMAN?

One of the earliest descriptions of these "wild men" was written in Arabic in the 12th century. It describes a creature that was said to live on the plains of Turkestan. It said the creature stood upright on two legs, like a human. The writer of the description thought that this creature was nearly human.

In several Arabic languages this creature is called the Almas. This is what it is now called. During the 19th century other reports of the Almas began to be written. It seemed to be something like the Wildman of China. It was said to be about the same height as humans, but covered with dark or reddish hair. It had long arms, and walked with the legs bent. The forehead sloped back from a bony ridge over the eyes. It had a large lower jaw, but not much chin. It had big feet, with wide, spoon-shaped toes, while its hands were humanlike, but with long fingers.

Around 1910 a Kazakh herdsman in west central Asia met with Russian zoologist V.A. Khaklov. The Kazakh said he had watched a female Almas for several weeks. She had been captured by some farmers. Later she was set free. The herdsman described how she behaved: "This creature was usually quite silent, but she screeched and bared her teeth on being

This Kazakh herdsman has rescued a sheep from the winter snow. Several herdsmen claimed to have seen Almas while rounding up their flocks.

approached. She had a peculiar way of lying down, or sleeping. She squatted on her knees and elbows, resting her forehead on the ground. Her hands were folded over the back of her head. She would eat only raw meat, some vegetables, and grain, and sometimes insects that she caught. When drinking water, she would lap in animal fashion, or sometimes dip her arm into the water and lick her fur."

" . . . he can pick up a chair, with a man sitting in it, with his teeth."

BORIS PORSHNEV

THE STORY OF ZANA

The strangest tale of all concerns a female Almas named Zana. She was captured somewhere in central Asia in the late 19th century. After some time she came into the hands of a Russian farmer named Edgi Genaba. At first, she was very wild and had to be watched night and day. After several years, however, she became tamer and was allowed to roam free.

Zana was large and very strong. Her skin was covered with reddish-black hair. She had a large jaw and big teeth, high cheekbones, and a flat nose. She never learned to talk, but muttered to herself. However, she could carry out jobs on her master's orders. When she was alone, she would spend hours banging and grinding stones together. She had her first child by a local villager. When it was born, she carried it to the river to wash it. But the baby could not stand the coldness of the water, and died. After that, the villagers took her children away from her when they were first born so that they could be looked after. It was said that Zana had two sons and two daughters that lived.

In 1964 a Russian scientist named Boris Porshnev visited the village. He wanted to collect what information he could about Zana. He was told that her youngest son, Khvit, had been a farmer. He was "extremely strong, difficult to deal with, and wild." Khvit seemed to be restless and uncontrollable.

LIVING RELATIONS

Porshnev also met two people who claimed they were Zana's grandchildren. From the time he saw them he was surprised by the way they looked. "Shalikula, the grandson, has unusually powerful jaw muscles, and he can pick up a chair, with a man sitting in it, with his teeth."

Professor Boris Porshnev in his study. He is holding the plaster cast of a giant footprint found in central Asia.

Over the next few years Professor Porshnev spent time in the overgrown village cemetery. He wanted to discover Zana's remains. He was not successful, but at last he found a skull, which he believed to be that of her youngest son Khvit. The skull had a very large, powerful lower jaw. Porshnev was convinced that it showed the features of a prehistoric human that was known as Neanderthal.

23

These Neanderthal skulls were part of a special show at the American Museum of Natural History in 1984. Porshnev believed the Almas were Neanderthals.

Boris Porshnev was also extremely interested in the reports of the way in which Zana had knocked and ground stones together. He wondered if this had been an attempt to make tools out of stone.

NEANDERTHAL SURVIVORS

Just before his death in 1974, Professor Porshnev published an article in the science magazine titled *Current Anthropology*. He suggested that the Almas is a survivor of the prehistoric Neanderthal people. This idea was supported by Professor John Napier, an expert on primate biology—that is, the study of the group of mammals that includes humans, apes, and monkeys. Napier wrote that he thought it was possible the Almas were the descendants of Neanderthals from the last ice age.

In 1925, Russian military surgeons had made a detailed examination of a body that was said to be a dead Almas. It was of medium height and heavily built. There were no great differences between its skeleton and that of modern humans. However, the head was different. It had a sloping forehead, and its brow stuck out. The lower jaw was huge, and it had a short nose. This was like the remains of prehistoric Neanderthal people that have been discovered.

HUNTING FOR THE ALMAS

In more recent years a scientist named Marie-Jeanne Koffman spent a long time collecting reports about the Almas. She collected dozens of stories from many people who claimed to have seen the creature in the Caucasus Mountains of southwest Russia.

In one, no less than 30 people told how they had seen an Almas eating corncobs in a field. Koffman's team found a line of footprints in the field and made plaster casts of the tracks. They also found two Almas caves that contained mounds of potatoes and fruits. Some had the marks of humanlike teeth on them. These marks showed that the teeth must have been set in a jaw slightly wider than most human jaws.

Koffman believes that this creature still exists, but that human activity in the area is threatening its continued survival. It is almost certain that no living Almas have ever been found and saved, like Przewalski's horse was. Until a living creature is captured so that scientists can study it, we will never know the real truth about the Almas.

Scientist Igor Burtsev with a cast of a giant footprint that was found in 1979. Others are still being found.

25

Bigfoot of North America

Perhaps the most famous of the giant humanlike beasts is Bigfoot. It is the only one said to have been filmed.

On the afternoon of October 20, 1967, Roger Patterson and his friend Bob Gimlin were riding their horses through the wooded highlands of northern California, near the border with Oregon. They were headed northward alongside Bluff Creek, a shallow waterway that flows into the Klamath River.

Just ahead was a tangle of logs and fallen trees, about 15 feet (4.5 m) high. As the riders reached it, a huge hairy figure stood up on the other side of the creek. The horses snorted with fear, rearing and backing. Patterson was thrown from his saddle. The creature began to stride away.

CAUGHT ON FILM

Patterson had a small movie camera in his saddlebag. Quickly he yanked it out. Plunging through the wet sand, he began to film, trying to keep the camera aimed at the creature. It turned to look at him and then disappeared into the undergrowth. And, at the same moment, Patterson discovered that he had run out of film.

The horses had run away, and it took the two men nearly an hour to find them. When they returned to the creek, the creature was long

Roger Patterson showed experts the film he had made of Bigfoot in 1967 (opposite). Many people thought the film was real. Others, however, were not so sure.

26

It turned to look at him and then disappeared into the undergrowth.

This is Roger Patterson holding two plaster casts of huge footprints. The photograph was taken within hours of his filming Bigfoot in October 1967.

gone. But there were footprints in the sand. Patterson and Gimlin were able to make plaster casts of them. They were 14½ inches (36.8 cm) long and 5 inches (12.7 cm) wide. The length of the creature's single step was some 40 inches (101.6 cm).

FEMALE BIGFOOT

When the film was developed, Patterson found he had about 24 feet (7.3 m) of footage. It ran for about a minute. It was jumpy and difficult to make out at first. But there was no doubt what it showed—a heavily built creature.

The creature was obviously a female. She had reddish-black hair all over her body, except for her lower face, the palms of her hands, and the soles of her feet. Her head seemed to grow right into her shoulders, without a neck. And her forehead sloped back to a high point at the back of her head.

She had thick arms, longer than a human's. Her legs were powerful. She walked with them bent. In fact, she looked something like a gorilla. Patterson and Gimlin claimed that they had taken the first moving pictures of the creature known in legends as Bigfoot.

SIGHTINGS OF BIGFOOT

Native Americans have told stories of "Bigfoot" (known as Sasquatch—"hairy giant"—in Canada) for centuries. Like the yeti, the Wildman, and the Almas, Bigfoot is tall, heavily built, and covered with reddish-black hair. It gets its popular name from the huge footprints that it leaves. Most sightings of the creature have been in the wild country of the northwestern United States, or across the border with Canada in

A thick forest in British Columbia, Canada. Most sightings of the Sasquatch have been reported in British Columbia.

British Columbia. In 1884 a British Columbia newspaper, the *Daily Colonist*, carried a story about the capture of one creature. The Sasquatch was spotted by the crew of a train, traveling between the towns of Lytton and Yale. They stopped the train and gave chase. The being they captured was built like a gorilla and covered with blackish hair. They called it Jacko. Jacko was put on show in the region, and then (it is said) was sold to the Barnum & Bailey Circus.

MEETING THE FAMILY

During the early 1900s more reports of sightings began to appear. Then, in 1924, a Canadian logger had an amazing experience. His name was Albert Ostman. He was worried that people would think he was crazy, so he didn't tell his story for 33 years. Then, on August 20, 1957, he took an oath, promising to tell the truth, before a court official at Fort Langley,

Albert Ostman (on the right) received many visits from journalists in 1957.
In August of that year he told how a Bigfoot had taken him prisoner in 1924.

British Columbia. According to Ostman, he had been camping near the head of Toba Inlet, opposite Vancouver Island. One night he woke up to find himself being carried inside his sleeping bag "like a sack of potatoes. The only thing in sight was a huge hand, clutching the partly closed neck of the bag."

Patterson and Gimlin claimed that they had taken the first moving pictures of . . . Bigfoot.

When Ostman was finally dumped on the ground, he found himself in the middle of a family of four Bigfeet. He claimed that the father of the family was 8 feet (2.5 m) tall, and the mother was about 7 feet (2 m) tall. There was what appeared to be a "teenage" son and a younger daughter. During the day the females searched for food. They brought sweet grass, different roots, and the fresh tips of pine and spruce trees. Meanwhile, the male bigfeet kept watch on Albert Ostman. The logger said he was kept prisoner for six days before he managed to escape.

SEARCHING FOR BIGFOOT

Albert Ostman's story finally came out at a time when there was still great popular interest in Eric Shipton's photograph of yeti tracks in the Himalaya Mountains. The story caught the interest of a Canadian newspaper man named John Green. He joined forces with a Swiss-born Canadian named René Dahinden. The two men spent the best part of the next 30 years in search of Bigfoot.

CLOSE ENCOUNTER

In 1955, Dahinden had taken the statement of a trapper named William Roe. Roe had been exploring a deserted gold mine near Jasper, Alberta. There he saw a creature that, at first, he thought was a grizzly bear: "Then I saw it was not a bear. My first impression [understanding of what he saw] was of a huge man, about 6 feet [1.8 m] tall, almost 3 feet [0.9 m] wide, and probably weighing near 300 pounds [136 kg]. It was covered from head to foot with dark brown, silver-tipped hair." Roe watched the creature as it came closer. It squatted and began to strip leaves from some branches.

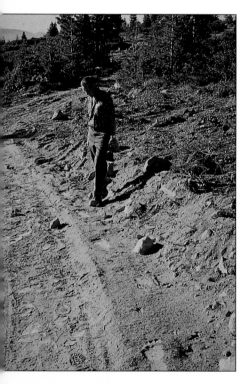

René Dahinden beside a trail of giant footprints in California on August 29, 1967. Two months later, Patterson made his film of Bigfoot at Bluff Creek, just five miles (8 km) from where these footprints were found.

A TIMID BEAST

Suddenly the creature spotted Roe, who said: "A look of amazement crossed its face. Still in a crouched position, it backed up three or four steps, then straightened up to its full height." The trapper said he thought about shooting the beast. However, it was so humanlike that he was unable to raise his rifle. As it walked away, it made "a peculiar noise that seemed to be half laugh and half language."

This is a strip of the film that Patterson shot of Bigfoot in 1967. Each picture is called a frame. These frames were studied by experts to see if the film was a trick.

In the fall of 1958, John Green went to the Bluff Creek region of northern California to check out a new report that he had received. A work crew was building a road through the area. One morning a bulldozer operator named Jerry Crew found huge footprints by his machine. For two months the work crew found more tracks circling their heavy equipment. Jerry made casts of one set of footprints. They were 2 inches (5 cm) deep and 16 inches (41 cm) long.

EXAMINING THE FILM

In August 1967 more footprints were found in the same area. Then, in October, Patterson shot his famous movie footage of Bigfoot there. The film was shown on television and seen by millions of people. Most scientific experts said it was a hoax, or trick—they said it was probably a man dressed in a gorilla suit.

Much of the discussion about whether the film was a trick or not centered around the speed at which it had been shot. The normal speed for movies is 24 frames per second (fps). A British expert, Donald W. Grieve, said

33

These Bigfoot footprints were found by a group of elk hunters on Coleman Ridge near Ellensburg, Washington State, on November 6, 1970.

that at this speed the creature appeared to move like a human. This would mean that the figure was probably a man in a gorilla suit. However, Grieve also went on to say that if the speed of Patterson's film had actually been set at 16 or 18 fps, then the creature must be real. At the slower film speed, said Grieve, it would be impossible for a human to move like the figure on the film. Roger Patterson was unable to remember the setting of his camera, but he thought it might have been running at 18 fps. Later, Russian scientists in Moscow tried a clever experiment. They measured the way the camera bobbed up and down as Patterson ran forward. At 24 fps, they said, he would have taken six strides per second. This is faster than a world-class sprinter. The experts decided the film must have been running at about 16 fps. Therefore, it was not a hoax.

NO ZIPPER!

Roger Patterson died in 1972, but the experts still continue to question whether the film was a trick or not. Shortly after Patterson's death, René Dahinden took the film to the Walt Disney studios. Disney films are famous for their animated animal characters. They are experts in movie trickery. However, people at the Disney studios said they could not have created a hoax so well. If the figure was a human dressed as a gorilla, nobody has yet discovered what film people call "the zipper in the suit."

OTHER SIGHTINGS

Between June 1964 and December 1970 alone, 25 separate Bigfoot sightings were reported. The total number of reported accounts of giant footprints and living creatures now runs into thousands.

This photograph was taken with a telephoto lens. It shows what appears to be a hairy, humanlike beast. The picture was taken in Spokane, Washington, on May 24, 1973. The photographer was 280 yards (256 m) away.

During the late 1960s, John Napier was a professor in Washington, D.C. Later, he worked at the University of London. In early 1972 he published a book about Bigfoot. In it he said: "No one doubts that some of the footprints are hoaxes. . . ." However, he also went on to say that if any one of the reports turned out to be true, then the matter would have to be taken very seriously. Finally, Napier wrote: "Some of the tracks are real. Sasquatch exists!"

35

Minnesota Iceman

In 1968 an amazing story came to light. It was about a huge humanlike creature found in a block of ice.

In his book about Bigfoot and other creatures, John Napier said that Bigfoot existed. However, he also noted that some sightings were tricks. Among the cases that Napier listed as tricks was the case of the "Minnesota Iceman."

Ivan T. Sanderson and Bernard Heuvelmans were zoologists, or scientists who study animals. Sanderson had taken a great interest in stories of yeti and Bigfoot. Heuvelmans was particularly interested in sea creatures, such as the giant squid and the legendary sea serpent. On December 9, 1968, Sanderson received a telephone call from Terry Cullen, a snake salesman in Milwaukee. Cullen told Sanderson about a man named Frank Hansen. He had shown a strange, apelike creature at a Chicago livestock fair. It was frozen into a block of ice. Then he had traveled around the Midwest, showing it at carnivals.

Sanderson and Heuvelmans drove to Hansen's farm near Winona, Minnesota, on December 17. A trailer was parked near the farmhouse. Inside the trailer was a large freezer cabinet. It contained a large block of ice. Frozen in the ice was a creature that looked like a man covered with long brown hair.

This is a photograph of Frank Hansen's Minnesota Iceman (opposite). Was he a real creature, or just a clever trick?

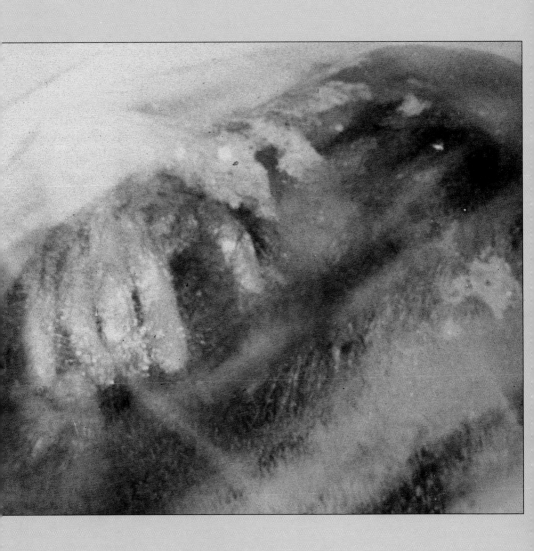

Hansen had shown a strange, apelike creature at a Chicago livestock fair. It was frozen into a block of ice.

Hansen's freezer, containing the Iceman on public display in a shopping mall.

AN AMAZING FIND

Sanderson and Heuvelmans spent three days drawing and photographing the creature. The ice was thick, and in places it was covered with frost. Sanderson had to lie on top of the glass top of the freezer to draw the creature. It was difficult to take good photographs.

The creature had no hair on its face. It was male, and its left arm was thrown up above its head. In a report the scientists wrote that "the creature is somewhat pug-faced, the tip of the nose turning inward. The forehead is sloping. The mouth is slit-like."

But where had the creature come from? Hansen told various, confusing stories. At first, he said it had been found floating in a 6,000 pound (2,724 kg) block of ice off the coast of Siberia. Later, it had turned up in the warehouse of a salesman in Hong Kong. It was then bought by a millionaire who lived in California. Hansen would not give the name. He said he had borrowed the creature from the millionaire. A year later Hansen told a different tale. He said he had shot the creature in Minnesota in 1961.

38

However, Heuvelmans decided that the "Iceman" had survived from prehistory. He named the creature *Homo pongoides* ("apelike man"). The report appeared in a Belgian newspaper on March 19, 1969. Soon the news had traveled all over the world.

The Smithsonian Institution, in Washington D.C., wanted to see the creature, but Hansen said he had returned the Iceman to its millionaire owner. He claimed that his creature was just a model of the real one. Eventually, however, Hansen did let experts from the Smithsonian look in his freezer. The frost was cleared away and new photographs were taken.

NEANDERTHAL CONNECTION

Sanderson and the Smithsonian did further detective work. Three companies each claimed to have made a model for Hansen in 1967. Some years later, in 1981, a Rhode Island newspaper claimed that the figure had been made by a Disneyland artist named Howard Ball. Ball's widow said this was true.

The creature had no hair on its face. . . . its left arm was thrown up above its head.

Bernard Heuvelmans refused to believe this story. He was certain that the creature was a Neanderthal (*Homo sapiens neanderthalensis*), which were prehistoric humans. In 1974 Heuvelmans and Professor Boris Porschnev, who had studied the stories of other giant, hairy creatures called Almas, wrote a book together. Its title was *The Neanderthal Man Is Still Alive*.

Neanderthal Survivors?

In 1997 a scientist came up with a new idea. Could it connect prehistoric humans to the stories of giant, humanlike beasts?

This head (opposite) shows what a Neanderthal woman might have looked like. The model was based on the measurements of a 41,000-year-old skull.

Neanderthals were prehistoric humans. They were named after the Neander Valley, which is not far from Düsseldorf in Germany. This area is where the first remains of an ancient humanlike skeleton were discovered in 1856. Since then more remains have been found in Europe, Asia, and along the North African coast.

Anthropologists are scientists who study the origin, history, customs, and beliefs of humans. They have worked out that Neanderthals lived about 200,000 to 30,000 years ago. Neanderthal skulls have thick browridges, large teeth, a huge jaw, and small cheekbones. They had powerful bodies, with large feet and hands.

DETECTIVE WORK

Until recently, anthropologists believed that the Neanderthals had gradually died out. They were followed by a different human species, the Cro-Magnons. Now, however, some experts have come up with a different idea. They believe it is possible that Neanderthals interbred with the Cro-Magnons some 30,000 years ago. In 1997, Professor Chris Stringer, from London's Natural History Museum, made an important suggestion

40

Until recently, anthropologists believed that the Neanderthals had gradually died out.

about DNA. DNA is a chemical found in the cells of every living thing. DNA is made of long strands. Sections of DNA, called genes, determine all of the physical characteristics of an individual. Specific genes in a certain order make a bird a bird and a human, human. Copies of genes are passed to offspring from their parents. This is why children often look like one or both of their parents or sometimes their grandparents. By comparing sections of DNA, an expert can trace genes from a child back to the mother and father and even earlier generations.

The prehistoric man . . . was a distant ancestor of the schoolteacher!

LIVING GENES

A few years ago researchers in England made an exciting discovery. They took DNA from the bones of a prehistoric man. Then they tried to find tiny pieces of matching DNA in people who still lived in the same area. They tested local schoolchildren, but they had no success. Then they tested the children's teacher. He had lived in the area all his life. There was no doubt. The prehistoric man who had lived there thousands of years before was a distant ancestor of the schoolteacher!

Professor Stringer had suggested that it might be possible to find traces of Neanderthal DNA in living people. This would prove that Neanderthals had not died out. Perhaps, he said, there are still such people living in wild, unexplored parts of the world.

Most reports of creatures, half-human and half-ape, come from eastern Asia. They cover the Himalayas, nearby southern China, and Mongolia. Even the frozen Minnesota Iceman may have come from there. According to one story told by Frank Hansen, who claimed that he had discovered the creature, the Minnesota Iceman had been found floating in a block of ice off the coast of Siberia.

ASIAN CONNECTIONS

In another of his stories of how he came across the beast, Hansen spoke of the body being found in a plastic bag. This was at the time of the Vietnam war, when the bodies of soldiers, sailors, and airmen were returned to the U.S. in "body bags." In November 1966, an article in the New York *World Journal Tribune* reported that Marines had been hunting in the thick forests. They shot tigers. "Other Marines," the article stated, "report that they shot a huge ape." But there are no known large apes in Vietnam, and

A forest in Vietnam. Some experts think that a Neanderthal might have walked from central Asia to Vietnam. There is, however, no proof of this.

although no Neanderthal bones have yet been found in Vietnam, it is possible that a surviving Neanderthal might have walked there from central Asia.

Was this the Iceman, and if so, was the creature a surviving Neanderthal? There are other facts to suggest that it might have been. One of the leaders of the Vietnamese National Liberation Front was Tran Dinh Minh. He told an Australian journalist about his experiences. One day he and some others saw tracks left by bare feet. They followed them and found a man sitting in a cave. He was covered with hair.

OTHER CONNECTIONS?

Strangely, there are still unusually hairy people living farther north, among the Japanese islands. These are called the Ainu. For hundreds of years the Ainu fought against the Japanese, until they were driven northward to the Hokkaido area. The Ainu have much more body hair than most other living human groups. Their language is unlike any other language.

However, most of the Ainu have now married people who are Japanese. There is no way of knowing what they once looked like. What is certain is that living Ainu do not look like Neanderthals.

But what about the North American Bigfoot? Could this be a Neanderthal?

Three Ainu fishermen in Japan. Ainu were once thought to be Neanderthal survivors.

This is a famous photograph. It shows the creature that François de Loys claimed to have killed in South America in 1917.

Millions of years ago all the continents of the world were joined together. Gradually the different pieces of land drifted apart. Even during the time of the Neanderthals, Alaska was still joined to Asia by a land bridge across the Bering Straits. Animals crossed over, and it is believed that Native Americans also came the same way. It is possible that some Neanderthals might have crossed over from Asia before them.

Around 1917 a scientific team led by Swiss scientist François de Loys was in the South American jungle—somewhere on the border of Colombia and Venezuela. They were attacked by apelike creatures and had to shoot one of them. Later they photographed the creature. It had a curiously humanlike face. It was over 5 feet (1.5 m) tall—much bigger than any known South American monkey. Later, in 1931, an Italian expedition collected stories people told about similar creatures.

BIGFOOT LIVES!

One scientist who believes that Bigfoot really exists is Grover Krantz, of Washington State University. His research into the creature began in 1969. He had soon collected more than 1,000 reports of sightings. Some people, he said, were "lying, were fooled by something else . . . or gave me information too poor to evaluate [decide one way or the other]. With the other half, I couldn't find anything wrong."

45

In June 1982, Paul Freeman was tracking a herd of elk near Walla Walla, Washington. Suddenly he saw a hairy figure about 60 yards (54 m) ahead. When it spotted him, the creature fled. Freeman found 21 clear footprints. He and Krantz made casts of them. Six days later they found another set of prints. Krantz decided they had been made by two different creatures. Both had feet about 15 inches (38 cm) long. The casts were so clear that he could see skin ridges (like fingerprints) on the soles of the feet. He said these would be impossible to fake. Since 1982 many more tracks have been found in the area.

NO REAL PROOF

So far nobody has produced a body—except the Minnesota Iceman, and that may be a trick. Some people who have seen Bigfoot say they did not want to shoot, because the creature appeared to be so human. So the mystery remains. Scientists such as Porshnev and Heuvelmans were sure that Neanderthals still lived. Many hunters have also been sure of what they saw. In wild areas of the world they claim to have seen and been watched by shy, hairy creatures. They move mostly at night, and they walk on two feet—like humans.

Grover Krantz (left) and Cliff Crook look at Bigfoot photographs at Bigfoot Central Headquarters in 1995.

46

Glossary

abominable Something that is unpleasant, below standard, or that causes great dislike. Abominable Snowman is the nickname of a giant humanlike beast said to live in the Himalayas.

academy A school that teaches a particular skill or subject. Also a group of experts working in the arts or sciences. For example, the Chinese Academy of Sciences.

advisors People who give other people, such as presidents and prime ministers, information or advice.

ancestor A member of the same family from a previous generation.

continent A great landmass such as Europe, Africa, or Asia.

descendant A member of a family following on from a previous generation of ancestors.

encounter A sudden, unexpected meeting with a person or thing.

examination Looking at something in detail. Also a task to test knowledge or ability.

exhausted Completely tired out, or something that has been completely used up.

expedition A trip or journey to find out about something.

footage An amount or length of film used in a camera.

genes Units that are inherited from parents which determine the characteristics of an offspring.

ice age A period of time when Earth was covered with ice.

ice ax A tool used to break up ice.

interbred Two different animal species that mate to produce young.

livestock Farm animals.

monastery A building where monks live and work.

Mongol A person from Mongolia, a country in East Central Asia.

plaster cast A copy of something made from plaster of paris, a quick-drying, chalky material that is mixed with water.

prehistoric A time before humans kept written historical records.

province An area within a country that makes its own rules and laws.

species A group of animals or plants that are similar and are able to mate and have offspring.

sprinter A person who runs short distances at high speed.

undergrowth Bushes, shrubs, and other low-lying plants.

zoologist A person who studies zoology, the science of animals.

Index

Further Reading

Bach, Julie S. Bigfoot, "Exploring the Unknown" series. Lucent Books, 1995
Coleman, Graham. Neanderthal. Gareth Stevens, 1996
Landau, Elaine. Sasquatch, Wild Man of the Woods, "Mysteries of Science" series. Millbrook Press, 1993
_____, _____. Yeti, Abominable Snowman of the Himalayas, "Mysteries of Science" series. Millbrook Press, 1993
Wayne, Kyra P. Quest for Bigfoot. Hancock House, 1996